MW00912881

Betty Roland was born Ma. town of Kaniva. Her first play, *The Touch of Silk*, made its debut at the Melbourne Repertory Theatre in 1928. Four years later she wrote the script of Australia's first talkie film, *The Spur of the Moment*. In 1933 she left an unhappy marriage and ran away with Guido Baracchi, a leader of the Australian Communist Party, who took her to Moscow. Her time there with Baracchi and Katharine Susannah Prichard is recounted in her Russian diary, *Caviar for Breakfast*.

After many years' involvement with left-wing politics and the New Theatre League, she began writing radio serials in 1942. She went to London in 1952 where her play *Granite Peak* was produced for television and where she wrote five books for children. Her publications include *Lesbos*, and the novels *The Other Side of Sunset* (1972), *No Ordinary Man* (1974) and *Beyond Capricorn* (1976). Returning to Australia, she settled at Montsalvat, where she wrote a study of the artists' colony *The Eye of the Beholder* (1984). The first volume of her autobiography was published in Imprint as *An Improbable Life* in 1989. *Caviar for Breakfast*, the second volume of her autobiography, was also published in Imprint in 1989.

IMPRINT

THE
DEVIOUS BEING

BETTY ROLAND

ANGUS
& ROBERTSON

A division of HarperCollins *Publishers*

AN ANGUS & ROBERTSON BOOK

Collins/Angus & Robertson Publishers Australia
A division of HarperCollins Publishers (Australia) Pty Limited
Unit 4, Eden Park, 31 Waterloo Road, North Ryde
NSW 2113, Australia

William Collins Publishers Ltd
31 View Road, Glenfield, Auckland 10, New Zealand

Angus & Robertson (UK)
16 Golden Square, London W1R 4BN, United Kingdom

National Library of Australia
Cataloguing-in-Publication data:

Roland, Betty, 1903-
   The devious being.

   ISBN 0 207 16698 6.

   1. Roland, Betty, 1903-   —Biography.
   2. Women authors, Australian—20th century—
   Biography. 3. Authors, Australian—20th century—
   Biography. I. Title.

A828.209

Typeset in 11/12pt Times Roman by Midland Typesetters
Printed in Australia by Globe Press
Cover photograph of Betty Roland by Jon Lewis

5   4   3   2   1
95 94 93 92 91 90

Nay, know ye not this burden hath always lain
On the devious being of woman;
Yea, burdens twain;
The burden of wild will and the burden of pain.

—EURIPIDES—

CHAPTER 1

In the first week in January 1935, the SS *Ballarat* berthed at Port Melbourne pier, almost two years to the day since she had sailed with Guido Baracchi and myself on board, en route to Moscow via London and the Baltic Sea.

We had planned to spend three weeks in the land of the Soviets, but, because of a fortunate sequence of events, had been able to extend that time to the greater part of two years. Now we were back where we had started, saddened to think that the great experience was over.

But not entirely. We were now committed to the task of winning as many converts to the Communist cause as lay within our power—confirmed as we were in the belief that the doctrines of Karl Marx and Friedrich Engels were the solution to the world's multiple ills. And the need for a solution had never been more urgent than in 1935.

The disastrous years of the Great Depression still afflicted the world economy; Hitler had set fire to the Reichstag and lit the furnaces of Auschwitz; the first shots of the Spanish Civil War were about to be fired, and every Marxist knew that this marked the beginning of World War II. That this opinion was shared by ever-increasing numbers of people was demonstrated by the dramatic rise in membership of the party of the hammer and sickle during the past two years, a phenomenon not confined to the downtrodden and oppressed as was to be expected, but embracing every colour, class and creed.

The hour indeed had come! Or so we believed in 1935, and to die on the barricades seemed an admirable thing to do.

Meanwhile, there were other and more immediate problems to be dealt with: Guido's wife, Neura, was standing on the wharf waiting to welcome us back home.

1

She had also been waiting on the wharf at Tilbury in 1933 when the *Ballarat* tied up, fully expecting to find him alone. When she had discovered I was with him, she had behaved in a quite exemplary manner. Far from shedding floods of tears and indulging in reproaches as the usual woman would do, she had given us her blessing and decided she would go back to Australia, also on the *Ballarat*! This magnanimous behaviour had impressed me very much and increased my regard for those who held Communist beliefs, but that regard was somewhat modified when, a few weeks later, she wrote to say that she was suing for divorce in order to marry Michael Hall, whom she had known in London and who had followed her to Australia.

This had shaken Guido rather badly, but had delighted me because it meant that he would soon be in a position to marry me, something I had scarcely dared to hope for. My hopes, however, were not fulfilled as neither the divorce nor Neura's marriage had taken place. She and Mike had had a row, he went off to Shanghai in a huff, and she had continued to occupy Guido's house in Darebin, a pleasant rural suburb in Melbourne, and was standing on the Port Melbourne wharf, prepared to welcome us and institute a ménage à trois between the three of us.

It was a bizarre situation that promised many hazards, and I had entertained misgivings but was in no position to protest, having cut myself adrift from both family and friends when I had abandoned my husband of ten years and a comfortable existence to embark on a perilous relationship with a man who was already noted for his lack of stability in his emotional relationships. Neura was not his first wife; before her there had been Kathleen, and a number of lesser women he had loved and left.

My hold on him was tenuous, and I knew it. I also knew that it would not help if I turned difficult and refused to share a communal roof with Neura. Guido loved the house on the river bank at Darebin—some of his best years had been spent there— and he was excited at the prospect of being there again, and might well refuse to follow me if I insisted on living somewhere

2

else. If I wanted him, and I most assuredly did, I must accept this ridiculous situation and make the best of it.

Guido's house, 'Larnoo', was in Riversdale Road, and though neither he nor Neura were aware of it, I had spent the first years of my married life in a house in the next street. In those days Darebin was a stronghold of respectability, and 'the Baracchis' were regarded with some suspicion, being 'known Communists' and also creating a disturbance from time to time by holding all-night parties, to which none of their neighbours were invited. On one occasion the sounds of revelry rose to such a pitch that the man who lived next door sent for the police and order was restored. His triumph, however, was short-lived, as not long afterwards, while he was burning off some rubbish in his garden, the wind veered round and set fire to Guido's paling fence. Guido sued for damages and was awarded fifty pounds. Thereafter there was open warfare between the two.

There were also Neura's prized Alsatian dogs, which took strong exception if anyone succumbed to curiosity and attempted to peer through the gap between the heavy gates that were always securely closed. This I discovered when I endeavoured to do so. Snarling and barking like the proverbial hounds of hell, they hurled themselves against the gate and threatened to break it down. I did not wait to see if they succeeded but hastened down the street pursued by the sound of their rage.

Now six years had elapsed and I was seated in Neura's car waiting for Guido to open those same gates and usher me into a new and totally different world.

There was no sign of the two ferocious dogs. They had died, suspected of being poisoned, while Neura was away and been replaced in her affections by a sweet-natured setter by the name of Mate, the warmth of whose welcome was in sharp contrast to the savagery of his Alsatian predecessors.

'Larnoo' was a comfortable old house with no claims to distinction apart from the acre of land on which it had been built and the river flowing at its foot. It reminded me of 'Lisonally', my grandfather's place in the Goulburn Valley in Victoria, where

3

I had spent my early childhood. They had been untroubled, happy years and I wondered if I would be able to say the same about my time at 'Larnoo'. I doubted it.

Guido and I were allotted a room at the rear of the house while Neura and Harriet, her niece, shared what could be termed the master bedroom in the front. I was unprepared for Harriet, and think that Guido was also taken by surprise when she came out to greet us. She was a handsome girl of seventeen or so and soon made it clear that she regarded me as an interloper whose early departure would be welcomed. Neura, on the other hand, went out of her way to be cordial and I responded in kind.

There was much to like about her; she was generous and warm-hearted. But she was given to sudden changes of mood that made her unpredictable. She also drank rather heavily at times and a curious change would overtake her face. It would lose its clear-cut lines, her lovely mouth grew slack and loose and her voice became strident and harsh. It was a transformation that I did not enjoy, but it appeared to leave Guido unmoved. He would listen to what she said, however outrageous it might be, nod his head and, like as not, refill her glass.

It was an explosive situation, not diminished by the arrival of Neura's elderly mother. She was a nice old soul who wandered about the place with a slightly bewildered expression and a strong suspicion that something rather odd was going on at 'Larnoo'. In other words, she distrusted me. Anxious to save her mother from distress, Neura had never told her that her marriage to Guido had broken down and my presence in the house was accounted for by saying that I was a relative who usually lived in Sydney! The poor old lady was only half-convinced and would look at me with an accusing expression in her faded eyes.

Bedtime became an exercise in deception. Despite all urgings to be reasonable, Neura's mother refused to go to bed at nine o'clock. 'I'm not tired,' she would say and continued to sit in her chair although already nodding off to sleep. Not until she had seen Guido and Neura securely shut in the conjugal bedroom would she consent to be led away to where she slept in the glassed-in porch at the rear of the house. Even then there was the risk that she would get out of bed to check that things were as they ought to be with regard to her daughter's marital affairs. So time had to be allowed to elapse before it was safe for Guido to creep down the hall to me. When Neura hit on the idea of giving her a glass of hot milk laced with brandy this stratagem became unnecessary.

The mad charade went on for quite some time, then Neura decided that she still loved Michael Hall and went off to join him in Shanghai. Harriet and her grandmother, more confused than ever, went back to where they had come from, and peace descended on 'Larnoo'.

There had been no further talk of a divorce, however.

CHAPTER 2

Guido had lost no time in re-establishing his bona fides with the Party after we returned. This entailed his writing a lengthy document, which took him days, in which he pleaded guilty to all the charges laid against him at the time he had opposed the official Party line. It was his *mea culpa*, and in time he was granted absolution and readmitted to the ranks of the true believers. It all seems rather childish now, but at the time it was deadly serious and Guido felt like Lazarus restored to health. Woman-like, I accepted everything he said, and received my Party ticket at the same time he was granted his.

From that time on we were deeply involved in party activities. Guido was given the task of setting up a series of Marxist classes, of which he was the tutor, and I was given the challenging task of establishing a workers' theatre. It was a clear case of making bricks without straw, as there was neither money nor venue, nor actors nor suitable plays with which to carry out this praiseworthy project. There was no lack of eager volunteers, especially for leading roles; the difficulty lay in the fact that few had any acting experience, and most had voices that were barely audible and suffered from stage fright. But it was my first assignment as a Party member and I was determined not to fail.

The Friends of the Soviet Union (FOSU) had a room somewhere in Lonsdale Street and let us use it for rehearsals, and eventually, after overcoming endless difficulty, we put on our first performance. It was an outstanding success and consisted of two short sketches written by myself and an extract from *Love on the Dole*. This was followed by other somewhat rough-and-ready productions and, growing more ambitious, *Waiting for Lefty* was being rehearsed when I was carried off to hospital to have my appendix removed and a quite remarkable young woman took over. Catherine Duncan was a student at Melbourne University who also attended one of Guido's Marxist classes, but whether her motive for being there was her interest in politics or passion for one of the other students, whom she eventually married, was a matter for debate. But that she was an extremely gifted actress and a writer of considerable talent is beyond dispute.

She welded my stumbling group of amateurs into something very like professionals, and when *Waiting for Lefty* was banned from the Collingwood Town Hall on the grounds of its Communist bias she made history by having it performed on the back of a large lorry in Hoddle Street before a crowd of several thousand sympathisers who would otherwise have never heard of it. It made headlines in the press, and the modest company formed in the FOSU rooms was soon to blossom into the New Theatre League, later the New Theatre, which, with its counterpart in Sydney, has flourished for over fifty years.

In addition to the Marxist classes and the Workers' Theatre, Guido and I were given less exalted party work to do. We stood at factory gates and on street corners selling copies of the *Workers' Voice* as well as delivering them to regular subscribers. We painted slogans on city walls and railway stations, stood on wooden crates and shouted our message to indifferent crowds on Friday nights when the shops stayed open till nine o'clock, attended rallies and marched with the unemployed. Once we were told to deliver incendiary leaflets to a military camp near Seymour, which might have earned us both a prison sentence for spreading sedition among His Majesty's forces, but it passed off tamely enough, as we took the precaution of choosing our time and tossing them over the barbed-wire fence when no-one was about and beating a hasty retreat. Not heroic, but we had done as we were told.

'Larnoo' became a convenient place for holding party meetings and for visiting delegates to stay in. The legend of Guido's wealth resulted in a levy that left us rather short of funds; I had to cook and make the beds and wash the sheets when our guests had gone, but was happy, having found a cause I could believe in and a man I could respect and love.

There was also the house and garden, both of which I loved. The garden had been neglected and with the help of one of the comrades (unemployed) I cleared away the weeds and replaced them with bulbs and annuals, dug a new bed and planted it with roses. There was a huge bed of Japanese iris languishing on the riverbank, overgrown and forgotten. They too were set free to reveal their glory when their season came. I have never had such a garden, either before or since.

There was also Guido's collection of books. They lined the walls of the living-room, row upon row of them, perhaps a thousand books, it could be more. And the Norman Lindsay etchings! Voluptuous nudes of nymphs and satyrs, bacchantes and obscene old centaurs romping in sylvan glades. A large oil painting of pirates, presumably on the Spanish Main, hung above the fireplace, but that was by Ray, Lindsay's son, and lacked the master's skill. There was a deep cushioned couch in front of the fire where one could read or fall asleep, with the red setter, Mate, dozing on the hearthrug and the smell of a burning log like incense in the air.

There was a Canadian canoe in the boatshed near the bed of irises, and on summer evenings we would sometimes drift along the river, a river that bore no resemblance to the sluggish stream that flows under Princes Bridge and is the source of much derision on the part of those who have never seen its upper reaches, where the trees are reflected in its placid water, or smelt the fragrance of the sassafras and aromatic shrubs that grow along its banks. We swam in it as well, Mate paddling beside us, looking slightly anxious. Once he lost his nerve and tried to clamber onto my back; I am an indifferent swimmer and swallowed several mouthfuls of the Yarra before I shook him off.

It was all too good to last, and came to an end when Neura wrote from London to say that she was coming home again as she and Mike had had another row. They had travelled from Shanghai by way of the Trans-Siberian railway, a test of endurance under any circumstances, but she was also ill, having contracted some obscure disease while still in China, and had spent some time in the London Hospital for Tropical Diseases. All of which had put too much strain on the fragile relationship between herself and Mike, so they had agreed to part, Mike to go back to Canada, from where he had originally come, and Neura to 'Larnoo'.

It was reasonable for her to want to do so. After all, the place was hers, Guido having transferred it to her along with a lot of other things by way of compensation for leaving her because of me. Which fact effectively stifled any protest that I might otherwise have made and gave us no alternative other than to vacate the room with the commodious double bed and pastel walls and resume our place in the room with the creaking iron bedstead and linoleum-covered floor.

But when Harriet also reappeared it was a bit too much even for Guido, so we hired a caravan, hitched it to the tow bar of our car and set out on a journey that took us through the forests of East Gippsland and the magnificent coast of southern New South Wales. It was a second honeymoon. We took Mate along with us and he was almost as ecstatic as ourselves, hanging his head out the window, long ears flapping in the wind, going crazy when he saw a rabbit or a cow. Once a wallaby hopped across our path and he went completely out of his mind, and had to be restrained when he tried to scramble onto the road and was severely scolded before he settled down again.

We got as far as Bateman's Bay, having loitered on the way, sometimes for a day or so at a particularly enticing spot. One of them was Mallacoota Inlet where we paused for a few days, held captive by the golden beaches and brilliant blue of the sea. When the fishing fleet came in, late in the afternoon, we bought shining silver fish and grilled them over a driftwood fire. Some of the locals came to talk to us and were invited inside the caravan to have a drink, but when Guido started to spread a little Communist propaganda they looked uncomfortable and said good night.

By the time we got to Bateman's Bay we had been on the road for the better part of a month and felt that it was time to turn back south again. But first I had a mission to accomplish.

I wanted to visit Twofold Bay and pay my respects to the memory of Benjamin Boyd, who had hoped to found a thriving city there.

Ben Boyd was a member of the London Stock Exchange who had astonished Sydney by arriving in his yacht the *Wanderer* in 1842 with an entourage of servants, an artist to paint a record of the voyage, a grand piano in the saloon and many other signs of limitless wealth. After being fêted like a conqueror and persuading many of Sydney's prominent citizens to take shares in his company, he proceeded to acquire immense tracts of land on the Monaro tableland, establish a whaling fleet to operate out of Twofold Bay, and draw up plans for the future city that he confidently hoped would eventuate from these and other enterprises. Not surprisingly, it was to be known as Boydtown.

He might have succeeded had not ill luck brought about his ruin. Violent storms destroyed a number of his whaling boats, and one of his merchant vessels, on its way from London, laden to the gunnels with urgently needed supplies and even more urgently needed men to build Boyd's town and guard his flocks, foundered as it rounded the Cape of Good Hope. Lloyd's of London disputed the claim for insurance and Ben Boyd went to London to institute law proceedings. He lost the case and had to meet the costs. When gold was discovered in Australia in 1851 Boyd's shepherds and carpenters deserted him and went to seek their fortune on the diggings, leaving his town unbuilt and his flocks and herds untended. In desperation, he resorted to blackbirding natives from the Hebrides and other Pacific islands, who, poor devils, were sent to the Monaro to fend for themselves, without clothes or proper shelter to protect them from the bitter winter winds.

Those who survived rebelled and straggled down to Sydney where they were seized and herded onto a trading vessel, to be dumped on some convenient island, where they were promptly speared by the indignant natives, who regarded them as enemies.

This was the end of Ben Boyd's dream of an Australian empire. He was bankrupt and disgraced; all that was left of his former affluence was his yacht *Wanderer*, which his creditors allowed him to retain. Always an optimist, he sailed to California in an attempt to mend his fortunes on the goldfields. Meeting with no success, he sailed back to the Pacific where, against his crew's advice, he went ashore on the island of Guadalcanal to shoot some game. A single shot was heard, but Ben Boyd was never seen again.

Ben Boyd was an adventurer on the grand scale—a bit of a rogue perhaps, but his story had fired my imagination. I had attempted to write a play about him, but he had proved too robust a character for me to grapple with so I had compromised by writing a play for radio, which was broadcast by the ABC on a single occasion and then consigned to oblivion. But Ben Boyd is not forgotten and Boydtown still stands on Twofold Bay, though it in no way resembles the bustling city he had visualised so confidently.

It is a popular camping ground today, but when Guido and I were there in 1935 it was a ghostly place with a ruined inn, a roofless church and a lighthouse whose beacon had never been lit to guide a sailor safe to port. It stood on the headland, silent and forlorn.

We camped in the lee of the ruined Seahorse Inn and explored its empty rooms, startling a family of possums that had set up house in its rafters. There were still relics of what had been the taproom, the remains of a bar, and at the back of it a windowless cell where, presumably, the drunks had been deposited for the night when they became obstreperous. Outside there were the relics of the vats in which blubber had been rendered into oil, but nothing remained of the pier at which the whalers and trading ships had tied up when they made port.

There was a moon that night and we climbed the hill that was crowned by the ruined church. Its roof had fallen in and a tree had sprouted where the pews had formerly been. It was a melancholy place, haunted by the ghosts of long departed worshippers and defeated hopes.

That was the night in which I discovered that my trusty contraceptive was not in its usual place, and when I asked Guido if he had thrown it away he admitted that he had. 'Do you want to make me pregnant?' I enquired indignantly. He gave me a mischievous smile and answered that he did.

I find it difficult to describe my feelings when I heard those words. Ever since poor little Peter had died six years ago, I had longed for another child to take his place, but had not succeeded in finding the man I would wish to be its father until Guido came along. But I had put the thought aside, because I felt he would not welcome the idea. He already had two children, one by an early marriage, the second by the luckless Isobel, in neither of which he took any interest, so why would he want a third? Now he had deliberately taken measures to show me I was wrong and I was overcome with joy.

There was more than one reason for this, among them my fear of Neura. This had increased since her breach with Michael Hall and her return to 'Larnoo'. I felt that her failure to marry Mike was because she was still in love with Guido and hoped to get him back. Her chances of this would be reduced if I should have his child, I told myself, a thing she had not been able to do. It was on this optimistic note that I faced a confrontation at 'Larnoo'.

Neura had watched us set out on our joyous holiday with a slightly wistful expression, but whatever sadness she felt at the time had entirely vanished by the time we got back. Mike had been reinstated in her affections and was already on his way back to Australia.

Next time I mentioned Sydney as a possibility, Guido thought it was a good idea.

CHAPTER 3

Since returning to Australia I had made no attempt to see any member of my family—even a chance encounter with an old friend was a thing I wanted to avoid—and had sometimes hinted to Guido that I would like to live in Sydney. He, however, had no wish to leave 'Larnoo'.

My wish to avoid everyone connected with my former life in Melbourne was largely due to a chance meeting with my austere Aunt Belle in London, another of those curious coincidences that had a marked effect on my life.

I had been standing in Oxford Street waiting for a bus that would take me to Maida Vale where Guido and I had been living since our return from the Soviet Union in the autumn of 1934. Bus after bus went past but none that would pass through Maida Vale, which was most unusual as there was usually one every few minutes. Finally, I decided to take the next one that went as far as Marble Arch and walk the remainder of the way. The next bus came along, I got on and took a seat and there, sitting opposite, was my Aunt Belle! We neither of us had the least idea that the other was in London and it took us a while to recover from our surprise.

There was no time for anything more than a few expressions of astonishment before we were at Marble Arch, where I got out, first having promised to see her that night at her hotel, somewhere in Bayswater; I cannot now recall its name.

Guido was reluctant to see me go, but I was excited at the thought of seeing somebody from home, even the aunt that I did not particularly like and rather feared.

The evening started pleasantly enough. Carefully avoiding any mention of Guido, she questioned me about the fifteen months in the Soviet Union, which she pointedly referred to as 'Russia', the events of 1917 being something she preferred to ignore. Finally came the crucial question: Now that I was back in the civilised world, what did I intend to do? I told her I was going back to Melbourne and would be sailing early in December.

'With that man Baracchi?'

'Yes, of course.'

Blood suffused her face, and I was subjected to a tirade of abuse that left me speechless. Had I no sense of decency at all? How could I have the effrontery to return to the place where I had disgraced myself so shamelessly? Did I not realise the sort of treatment I would receive? I would be ostracised, an outcast; nobody would want to speak to me. And on and on.

The attack was so unexpected, so ferocious, that there was nothing I could say. Finally she fell silent and I crept away, lacerated by that bitter tongue.

'I rather suspected something of the kind,' said Guido, trying to stem my hysterical tears when I got back to our hotel.

But even cold-hearted Aunt Belle felt she had gone too far. Shortly afterwards a letter came, in which she said she was sorry for having caused me such distress when I already had so much to contend with and that, if I would agree to leave Baracchi, she would return to Australia and prepare a place for me to come to—presumably in some secluded country retreat—until such time as he was in a position to marry me. Needless to say, I replied that I was quite happy as I was and that the answer was 'no'.

Following which, we spent some weeks in a picturesque stone cottage on the fringe of Bodmin Moor in Cornwall. It was autumn, the heather was in bloom, we bought homemade bread and clotted cream from a nearby farm, and London and my Aunt Belle seemed far away. Nevertheless, the lacerations had not fully healed and, when we got back to Melbourne, I was glad of the refuge provided by 'Larnoo' and the demands of party work, which prevented me from mourning the loss of family and friends.

The exceptions to this wish to avoid all contact with the past were the members of the Meldrum School, with whom I had always kept in contact, and particularly Lil and Justus Jorgensen, who had been my special friends. This rather exclusive little clique was as unorthodox in outlook and lifestyle as I was myself, so I had no need to fear a rebuff from them. But considerable changes had taken place in the two years that I had been away.

In 1933 Lil had reigned unchallenged in Justus's affections; now she had been displaced by a younger, prettier woman, which he made no effort to conceal from her. She still lived in the Brighton studio with Max, their son, but Jorgensen was rarely there, dividing his time between his studio in the city, where he taught painting during the week, and his weekends on a five-acre block of land at Eltham, where, with the aid of the more dedicated of his pupils, he was in the process of building a replica of a mediaeval village principally composed of mud bricks, pisé, and discarded scraps of timber scrounged from rubbish-tips and junkyards. He planned to call it Monsalvat ('my salvation'), and he and his disciples would live there in perfect harmony, practising art for art's sake and setting an example to the world. He also visualised a time when Helen, his new love, and Lil, his wife, would no longer resent each other and set another example to the world.

Guido and I were saddened by the change in Lil when we went to visit her in Brighton. She was her usual sunny self, but even her bright smile could not dispel the gloom of the deserted studio, which had once been so full of life and colour, nor conceal the fact that the cruel disease that had been barely hinted at two years ago (multiple sclerosis) now had her firmly in its grip. She swore that there was nothing seriously the matter with her, that the pins and needles in her hands and feet were due to bad circulation and that all she needed to do was get out of her chair and take more exercise. We hoped that she was right.

Max was now four years old, a lively little boy who made conversation difficult, so we cut the visit short, feeling that Jorgensen's dream of a harmonious community at Eltham was unlikely to be realised. Guido, however, was intrigued by the idea of communal living and, on a hot Sunday afternoon, we drove out to Eltham to see what progress had been made.

A group of men and girls was engaged in digging foundations, treading mudbricks and erecting scaffolding on the slope of a gently rising hill. They surveyed us rather coldly, as though regarding us as intruders. Jorgensen, in contrast, was fulsome in his welcome, shook hands warmly and said how glad he was to see us, after which he proceeded to outline his plans for what seemed like sheer fantasy.

Breaking off a piece of stick, he knelt and sketched the outlines of his dream. Here a row of student cubicles, in front of them a swimming pool, close by would be a communal dining-room, a good-sized kitchen and a storehouse. A flight of stairs would lead from this into a studio, which in turn would give access to an enormous Gothic hall, which was to be the ultimate achievement of the scheme. It would consist of several levels, have a musicians' gallery where stringed instruments would play Vivaldi, Bach and occasionally Mozart. It would be crowned by a pitched roof of slates—there was a large pile of them on the hill behind him (a donation from a rich admirer), one of his students was already learning how to make stained glass for the windows, two others were carving bosses and corbels and would later try their skill at hewing gargoyles out of the slabs of granite lying in the grass. A house for Lil was already under way.

We were mistaken in being sceptical. Those soaring dreams came true, and Montsalvat stands today as a monument to the man who achieved what appeared to be the impossible.

Early in January 1937, we were on our way to Sydney on the overnight express and I learned the difference between travelling as the wife of a successful businessman and travelling as the de facto wife of a dedicated Communist. Where I had formerly enjoyed the comfort of a sleeping berth, I now sat bolt upright on an unsprung seat with a crick in my neck and a feeling of slight ill-use, but I told myself that I was there from choice and therefore must not complain. For a Communist to travel 'first' was a disgrace, like wearing gloves—I had already been guilty of that on a bitter Melbourne day and been soundly reprimanded for doing so. Only the bourgeoisie wore gloves.

With the exception of the books, we had brought nothing from 'Larnoo'. Mate and the Norman Lindsay etchings, even the Morris Minor car, were left behind; we had our clothes and nothing else. The books filled eleven packing cases and were left in storage until we had found some place to live. As a temporary measure we rented a flat in Elizabeth Bay Road and started on our search. The choice was very wide, because the Depression had not fully lifted and there were flats and even houses lying vacant all over Sydney, even in Rose Bay, Vaucluse and Mosman, but though the rents by present standards were absurdly low, they were too high for us. So we settled on a flat in Balmain, on the very tip of Long Nose Point.

Balmain is now fashionable among the avant-garde of Sydney's young intelligentsia, real and pseudo, but when Guido and I moved into Louisa Road it was only slightly better than the slums of Surry Hills and distinctly working class. The rent was twenty-five shillings a week and for that we had the upper floor of a two-storey house with a magnificent view of the harbour and the bridge and at night the glittering lights of Luna Park.

Directly below our windows was a jetty where a busy little ferry called in on its way from Circular Quay to Hunters Hill, and a constant procession of coal barges, cargo ships and even the occasional naval vessel passed by, belching evil-smelling smoke from their diesel-burning bowels. The rank smell of burning oil was particularly hard on me as, shortly after we moved into Louisa Road, I discovered I was pregnant.

That changed everything. Balmain was the perfect base from which to pursue our political aims, but as a place in which to rear a child, especially this child, it was in no way suitable. This precious being must have unpolluted air, peace and beautiful surroundings in which to thrive. We found all three at Castlecrag, Walter Burley Griffin's answer to 'the creeping erysipelas of red-roofed suburbia'.

Burley Griffin had fallen in love with the Australian bush soon after his arrival from Chicago, and was appalled at the vandalism that was taking place, so, when the bureaucrats and politicians had succeeded in driving him out of Canberra, he turned to Castlecrag as a means of healing his wounded spirit. He formed a company called the Greater Sydney Development Association, in which he held the majority of shares, and purchased the entire headland, reducing himself to penury by doing so.

The land was subdivided, roads surveyed and For Sale signs went up but Griffin had put a covenant on the land that prohibited the felling of trees or any destruction unless it was needed to clear enough land for the house to be built. Furthermore, the house must not exceed a certain height, must not block its neighbour's view and must be built of stone, preferably quarried on the site, or else of concrete tiles called Knitlock, which Griffin had invented himself.

All very laudable, but the covenant had an inhibiting effect on any prospective buyer. Then the Depression came, and prices had fallen disastrously by the time Guido and I went out to select the site of our future home in 1937. Guido had always admired Burley Griffin—he had commissioned him to design a house to replace 'Larnoo', but it had not been built when his marriage to Neura had broken up—and it was natural that he should now feel attracted to Castlecrag. Griffin, poor man, had died in India early that year, and it was his partner, Eric Nicholls, who took us out to choose our block of land one Sunday afternoon.

Eric was an affable and extremely likeable man who went to great pains to show us all the blocks with the best views and in the least inaccessible positions before we finally made our choice. It was on the corner of The Bastion and The Bulwark— Griffin had named all the roads to represent some part of a mediaeval castle—and it cost us precisely £160.

Having made our selection, we were taken to one of the original Burley Griffin houses on The Parapet and given afternoon tea. Our hostess was a sweet-faced woman of middle years whose name was Ula and who possessed a great deal of charm. There was a husband somewhere who did not appear, and a lovely little girl who danced around the lawn with nothing but a mane of honey-coloured hair to hide her nakedness. I thought she was quite delightful and hoped I, too, would have a lovely little girl. I liked her mother also, and felt glad to think that I would have her as a neighbour when the house was built and we lived at Castlecrag.

She might even become the friend that I was hoping for.

CHAPTER 4

The time that can elapse between buying a block of land and taking possession of the house you build on it can be considerable, and in our case it was a full two years; a number of unforeseen events contributed to this. Meanwhile, we continued to live in Louisa Road, where other drawbacks apart from diesel-burning boats began to manifest themselves. There was the perennial shortage of cash, of course, which was no novelty to me, but it was a contributing cause to the purchase of a versatile piece of furniture in an auction room. By day it was a couch, by night it opened out and became a bed. It was a bargain and we were quite pleased with it, until the startling discovery that it was infested with bedbugs.

Now, while I had been prepared to accept the presence of the loathsome little beasts in the Soviet Union, they were totally unexpected in civilised, sanitary Sydney and it was not only the smell of burning diesel oil that made my stomach heave on the morning of the discovery. Even Guido looked a little perturbed. So we slept on the floor for the next few nights while the offending object was taken away to be de-bugged by a pest extermination company, whose minions arrived in a van emblazoned with a skull and crossbones, exposing our shame to all the neighbourhood.

'Don't worry, lady,' one of them said. 'You'd be surprised at the places we have to go to. Some of the toffiest houses in town. Sydney's alive with 'em, it being in the tropics, see?'

Guido scouted the idea, but I liked the thought of Sydney being in the tropics, and if bedbugs were the price of living there, there was also the view of the harbour and, above all else, the frangipani. January is the month when it is at its best and even the shabby streets of Balmain had their share of the flower-laden trees and the perfume, especially at night.

We had noisy neighbours. A large and tumultuous family occupied the lower floor. The children fought and screamed by day and their parents quarrelled violently at night. But the wife was a friendly soul, and in no time at all she was telling me her woes. One day I found a wedding ring embedded in the lawn below the house. 'Oh yes, it's mine,' she said. 'I threw it out the window to annoy Ted and never got around to looking for it.' She soon discovered that I was pregnant and we were sisters after that.

Eric Nicholls had agreed to design the house on Castlecrag and perhaps he realised that Long Nose Point was not the ideal place in which to spend the early weeks of pregnancy as he announced one day that a nice little Burley Griffin house was about to become vacant and that, if we so chose, we could live there while our house was being built. We did not even ask to see it but transferred ourselves and our few possessions, including the decontaminated bed, to The House of Seven Lanterns, hidden away in a secluded cul-de-sac called The Barbette. After Louisa Road it was a haven of tranquillity, and I settled in to grow my baby in unclouded happiness.

So I had hoped, but events proved otherwise.

Eric Nicholls had been tardy in designing our future home, but when he finally laid his plans before us, we forgot our irritation. They were exciting and unusual, but when we heard how much they would cost to build, our faces fell, as it was far beyond our means. Eric went away and made some modifications, but the price was still too high. The circular room was the trouble, but it was the leitmotif of the whole house and without it we would have nothing but a conventional two-bedroomed house instead of one that was unique. Not only did it create structural problems, as nothing was standard, not even the folding doors, there was also the fireplace. Burley Griffin had always made a special feature of his fireplaces; they generally smoked, but they were the focal point of the house, round which the family would gather, tribal fashion. Eric, his loyal disciple, had carried on the tradition by designing a massive affair of honey-coloured

24

stone, hand hewn in the Hunter River valley, each block costing quite a tidy sum of money. Once more, we had to shake our heads, so Eric rolled up his plans and promised to think up something less spectacular at some later date. So it seemed as though we were going to live in The House of Seven Lanterns much longer than we had thought.

Then a miracle occurred.

In his early twenties Guido had married a girl called Kathleen, always known as Toby, causing considerable pain to two other young women who had hoped that he would marry one of them.

'Why did you marry Toby?' I asked him one time.

'Because she refused to go to bed with me unless I did,' was the cool reply. From which one can assume that the other aspirants had been less resistant to his charm.

In addition to being careful of her virtue, Toby had a brother-in-law who got into financial difficulties and borrowed a considerable sum of money from the youthful bridegroom, but even that was not enough to save him from bankruptcy, and Guido accepted the fact that the loan would never be repaid. But he had other problems at the time, having been sentenced to three months in Pentridge Gaol for having made an incendiary speech on the Yarra bank one Sunday afternoon, and Toby had taken the opportunity to run away to Sydney with a former boyfriend. Now, twenty years later, Guido met her brother-in-law in the street.

'Guido Baracchi!' said Bill. 'I've been looking for you everywhere. I want to get a discharge from the bankruptcy court and must pay all my bills.'

'Here's your house,' said Guido, handing me the cheque when he came home that night. It fell short of the required amount, but he overcame his aversion to going into debt and insured his life with the AMP Society, which then lent him enough to pay for the house.

It was at this point that Eric Nicholls came down to warn me about the titles to the land on which it was soon to be built. They had not been finalised, he said, and did I not think they should be registered in my name? This was something I had not thought about and looked surprised.

'If they're in Guido's name you'll have no claim on the house,' he went on.

'What does it matter?' I answered and began to cry.

The reason for my tears was Ula, the woman on The Parapet who had given us afternoon tea the day we bought the land. Guido had also succumbed to her charm and had developed the habit of calling in as he went past her house. At first he had said this was because he had hopes of inducing her to join the Party, but when the visits became more frequent and he sometimes spent whole evenings with her and took her to Party meetings, I protested. I was told that it was my duty as a Party member to encourage her and not give way to petty jealousy!

So what did I care about who owned the block of land? If Guido had fallen in love with another woman, nothing else mattered to me. Eric seemed to understand. He sat in silence for a while, then patted my hand and got up to go.

'Think it over,' he said. 'If you change your mind just let me know.' I did think it over, and the deeds were made out in my name.

Guido was now persona grata with the party, having admitted his mistake in holding contrary opinions to those advocated by the Kremlin and having sworn never to deviate again. He had been made co-editor of the *Communist Review*, the mouthpiece of the Party, and he took it very seriously. He also continued holding Marxist classes, as he had done in Melbourne, which required preparation, so with these and the time devoted to the *Review*, and recruiting Ula, there seemed little time left for me.

His classes and his work on the *Review* often occupied him till well after midnight, and I would be asleep by the time he came to bed. So, without any conscious planning, our physical relations ceased. This did not trouble me unduly, as pregnancy had reduced my libido to almost nil, and I told myself that things would return to normal after the baby was born. But I started

26

to sleep badly in the last three months and had to take a sleeping-pill in order to get the eight hours prescribed by Dr Truby King.

On the surface, everything appeared to be quite normal at The House of Seven Lanterns, and nobody on Castlecrag suspected that anything untoward was taking place between Mr and Mrs Baracchi and the nice woman on The Parapet.

Mrs Baracchi? No-one had the least suspicion that Guido and I were not married, and I saw no reason to tell them otherwise. It was a harmless enough deception and injured no-one, but it made things easier for me. I had a lot to cope with and felt unequal to the ordeal of facing my neighbours' disapproval, unspoken though it would probably be. Eric Nicholls was the exception. He had known Guido and Neura when they were together at 'Larnoo' and must have been very surprised when Guido appeared in Sydney with me. But beyond the time when he went out of his way to warn me about the title to the land on which the new house was to be built, he gave no indication of the fact that I was, in some ways, an imposter.

The baby, an exquisite little girl, was born on the morning of 13 October 1937, at five minutes after nine. It was not an easy birth, and it left me weak and shaken, but I was able to meet my obligations as a nursing mother and the baby thrived. Guido was delighted with her, concealing any disappointment that he may have felt that she was not a boy, but, engrossed as he was with Party work and, alas, Ula, he had little time for us. He would come hurrying in, kiss us both, then sit down and begin correcting proofs for the *Communist Review*, or notes for that night's Marxist class. No time to talk to me, no time to gloat over the baby.

I wrote notes to him, asking for any little thing I wanted him to bring for me. He did not bring me any flowers but brought me a copy of *Gone With the Wind*, which had just appeared, on the flyleaf of which he had written out a verse of the poem 'Cyrana'.

> *I have forgot much, Cyrana! gone with the wind,*
> *Flung roses, roses, riotously with the throng,*

Dancing, to put thy pale, lost lilies out of mind;
But I was desolate and sick of an old Passion,
Yea, all the time, because the dance was long:
I have been faithful to thee, Cyrana! in my fashion.

In his fashion! Was that all he could promise me? I read the book in search of words of comfort, but found none. Scarlett O'Hara lost her man, and I felt that she deserved to do so. But she became a symbol of endurance and survival and her words on the final page: 'I'll think about that tomorrow', became my guiding principle. So, when the nurse came in, put out the light, and took the book away in case I should read it half the night, I, too, turned over and fell asleep.

CHAPTER 5

Beyond a few half-hearted attempts to interest myself in communal affairs, such as the drama group and the reading circle, I had led a fairly isolated life at Castlecrag. I had little in common with the people living there, and was too engrossed in my own affairs to make further overtures, and they made no effort to get acquainted with me. The exception was Roberta Yardley.

She came dancing into my life when Gilda was a few weeks old. I say 'dancing' because she was very happy at the time and came down The Bastion towards me on feet that seemed to barely touch the ground. I had Gilda in my arms, wrapped in a fleecy shawl whose blue matched the colour of her eyes.

'Do let me see,' Roberta said, and drew aside the shawl. 'O-o-h, I simply *must* have a baby girl!'

I had not met her before and was charmed by her blonde prettiness, her joie de vivre, and the brightly coloured dirndl she was wearing. Dirndls were all the rage that year and this one showed off her pretty figure and slim waist to perfection. She might even have had a flower in her hair; I don't remember, but she often did.

The next thing I recall of her is in the Burley Griffin house in Edinburgh Road. It was one of the first he had built on Castlecrag and was particularly ugly, but it was the first home Roberta had ever had and she was delighted with it. She was in a happy mood that day as a new pair of blankets had just arrived. She cut the string and tore the wrapping aside, held them against her cheek, then threw herself down on the bed and wrapped herself in the apricot-coloured folds. She and Edgar were newly married and had made do with a sleeping-bag so far.

I think she was already pregnant, but I can't be sure, but when the baby came it was not the pretty little girl she hoped for but a boy, a robust, aggressive little male who refused to behave as a baby should; he disliked being cuddled, refused the breast and spat out the milk she gave him from a bottle, the upshot of which was that she became discouraged and refused to try any longer to break through his determined resistance to her. Edgar, his father, took over where she left off. He doted on his little son and had no difficulty with him at all.

Edgar was a Yorkshireman who had come out to Australia in the early days of the Depression. He was a skilled tradesman and a conscientious workman and had prospered reasonably well. He also had a secret ambition to go on the stage, which drew him into the orbit of the New Theatre League. He was unique in that he had a regular pay envelope and was willing to add a leg of lamb or pound of cheese to the depleted larder of the jobless who made the League their home. He was also known to be good for a 'touch' from time to time, which made him very popular. In addition, he was quite a gifted actor and ready to play all sorts of unsuitable roles, as well as knocking up a set in his spare time or painting a backdrop at a moment's notice.

In short, he was a thoroughly nice, good-natured sort of chap and just the type to fall besottedly in love with a woman like Roberta.

She, too, had secret ambitions to go on the stage, but had very little ability, so made herself useful by helping to make the costumes and brewing mugs of tea. She was allowed to attend rehearsals and sometimes sleep on one of the piles of hessian and dirty old carpets that had been scrounged from a junkyard by members of the League.

When she married Edgar she already had a child, a boy of five called Michael; she had been married to someone in Tasmania, where she had been born. She did not talk about this marriage very much, but I gathered from the little that she did say that it was a gentlemanly ne'er-do-well who fathered a child on her and left her to battle on as best she could. How or why she found her way to Sydney I do not know, but for one of Roberta's temperament it was the natural place for her to be. After Launceston it must have been a heady experience.

Unlike Edgar, she had no particular skill, but she did have a fine young body and few inhibitions, so it is not surprising that she gravitated towards the so-called 'bohemian set' of painters, poets and other colourful characters who congregated principally around Kings Cross. From them it was an easy transition to the studios of Norman Lindsay, Rayner Hoff, and the life class at the Sydney Gallery.

It was a precarious way to earn a living, but she thoroughly enjoyed it. In addition, Michael, from an early age, added his trifle to the family purse. He was a delicate child with a tendency to asthma but was also very beautiful, so he, too, stood motionless for hours on end while his cherubic body was modelled in wax or clay. He did not complain, but he suffered permanent damage as a consequence. His fragile bones were unequal to the strain, so that his knees gave way, and his legs were still in callipers when his mother met and married Edgar.

When I saw her coming down the hill towards me, she was radiantly happy. She was on her way to visit Frank and Anise Duncan, who lived in another early Burley Griffin house not far from ours. They had come out from England to escape the Great Depression and had bought the land and built the house for a modest £500. That was in 1933 and it proved to be a sound investment; in 1989, when it was sold, the price was an astounding half a million dollars. But Anise was not there to share in the bonanza; she had died some years before.

Frank and I had very little in common, but Anise had been two months pregnant when Guido and I moved into The House of Seven Lanterns and that had been enough to create a bond of sympathy between us. But there was never much more than that; she was a simple, guileless soul, totally overwhelmed by Frank, who was brusque and had a rather surly manner and did not appeal to me at all. They already had a son called Ross, a handsome, rather fragile-looking boy of six, who admired his father but was in awe of him. He was the apple of Frank's eye. The Duncans were ardent bushwalkers and used to go off on hikes at the weekend, bowed down by the weight of the packs they carried on their backs, and if Ross lagged behind and

31

complained of feeling tired, Frank showed him no pity and urged him to go on.

They were also vegetarians, and I listened in astonishment when Anise described the diet that she followed, even during pregnancy. It seemed to consist of fruit, vegetables, and a limited amount of cheese and eggs. Once, she ate no solids for several days and I found her lying limp and pale-faced under a tree and told her that the baby would suffer as a consequence. She smiled and shook her head, but I think I made some impression as she admitted eating a nut cutlet and some yogurt the following day.

I was the first to go into the labour ward at Crown Street Women's Hospital, and Anise followed suit soon afterwards, but she went to the Sanitarium at Wahroonga, where nut cutlets and meatless rissoles were *de rigueur* and patients were required to conceal their nakedness with a rubber apron whenever they took a bath. Comparing our respective offspring in the baby clinic later on, I was confirmed in my belief that a good substantial diet of red meat and three vegetables is a better basis for producing a robust child than nut meat rissoles and cottage cheese.

The stork was a constant visitor at Castlecrag that year; several babies arrived in quick succession. But there was one empty cradle that he failed to fill in spite of all inducements to do so.

The Heslings, Bernard and Flo, had also come out from England at the beginning of the war. Bernard had been here before and seen Castlecrag and thought that he would like to live there. But that time had not yet come, as he was homesick for the Yorkshire moors and his dear old Mum, so he went back home. He found it did not meet his expectations, met and married Flo and persuaded her to come to Sydney. At first they rented a Burley Griffin house at the top of the hill, just up from ours, then, as Bernard grew more prosperous, they purchased an arid block of land on the opposite side of the road. Burley Griffin was dead and had no say in the house that Bernard designed and built, so was not driven to frenzy by its pitched roof and stark white walls. But it did not block anybody's view and in place of planting trees, Bernard dug a swimming pool and planted cactus in a tub. He was immensely proud of it and never ceased to marvel at his luck in having such an impressive place in which to live. He also never ceased to marvel at his luck in having snared such a downy little bird as Flo.

'I've been married to her for years,' he said one time, 'and I'm just as mad about her as I ever was.'

'Making love to Flo is the most exciting thing I ever did,' he confided on another occasion. Then: 'Flo likes to wander round the house in the nuddy when it's hot, and if I see her bending down to pick something off the floor, I get worked up and just can't help myself'.

Never reticent, he indicated that he sometimes 'got worked up' several times a day. But still the stork refused to come their way. They tried every known method in an attempt to lure him into their nest. They consulted gynaecologists, psychologists, naturologists, read the Karma Sutra and Marie Stopes, resorted to Chinese herbalists and faith healers, but all to no result. Then Flo went into hospital to have something done to her tubes, and Bernard submitted himself to the indignity of a sperm count. This became a popular addition to his repertoire of after-dinner stories.

'They gave me a pyrex bowl,' he bitterly complained. 'I thought that was a little poor. I hadn't expected crystal but it might at least have been cut-glass.'

It was really a little sad, and Flo's infertility became a matter of concern to all her friends. When she shook her head at the end of each successive lunar phase, there was a genuine feeling of disappointment. But they had a surrogate in the form of an ever-pregnant cat called Harpie, who was the most ravaged animal that I have ever seen, only equalled by Picasso's she-goat in the New York Museum of Modern Art.

Flo and Bernard kept a record of her numerous offspring and at the latest count they numbered several hundred. When they went to Adelaide to live, they took poor Harpie with them, and one can only hope that the change of climate brought about her menopause.

Bernard prospered in Adelaide. He had already earned a considerable reputation in Sydney as a cartoonist and writer of humorous articles in the *Sydney Morning Herald* and the *Bulletin*. He also painted amusing pictures, which he sold to his admirers. But his crowning achievements were vitreous enamel trays and coffee tables, his unique contribution to art. Vitreous enamel is commonly used for gas stoves or the benches on a kitchen sink but, because of Bernard's inventive genius, it was called upon to fulfil a higher destiny.

This was the result of his having been commissioned to paint a mural on the exterior wall of a building in the city. He was to be paid a substantial sum, and gave the matter careful thought. When he had decided on a suitable design, he looked at it and thought that it was a pity that the sun and rain would wash it all away. Then he remembered some advertisements that he had seen on railway stations in England, dozens of them, all apparently indestructible and all in vitreous enamel, which, being an amalgam of pigment, ground glass and linseed oil, is impervious to even the most inclement weather. So the bank got its mural, and Bernard discovered a new and lucrative source of income.

He painted landscapes and scenes of Sydney Harbour in the new medium, but they hung fire, so he took them out of the frames and added a leg to each corner and, presto! he had coffee tables. They were an instant success, so he extended his range to enamel trays, many of which had poor Harpie's haggard face peering out from among the poinsettia flowers and futuristic designs with which he adorned them. Then someone persuaded him to go to Adelaide and hold an exhibition at the same time as the biannual festival.

Adelaide was delighted both with Bernard and with his trays and coffee tables; red seals blossomed like the floral clock on North Terrace and he decided that Adelaide was the place in which his future fortunes lay. So he returned to Castlecrag with an increased bank account and a firm resolve to sell the White House and transfer Flo and Harpie to the city of churches and culture.

Flo was less than enthusiastic, but finally they departed with what remained of their belongings packed into the back of a secondhand truck that Bernard had bought, with Harpie in a basket and Flo in tears.

Apart from the Heslings and Roberta, the only people living at Castlecrag with whom I felt any affinity were the Claridges, a couple who lived in another Burley Griffin house built within a few feet of The Seven Lanterns. They were an ill-matched pair; Ern was expansive, large and jovial while Win was small, tight-lipped, and tended to keep her feelings to herself. She was friendly enough to me though, and I was glad of the welcome I received whenever I dropped in for a drink and a yarn in the evening or on a Sunday afternoon. There were usually a number of other people there, as Ern was the soul of hospitality and liked nothing better than to sit in his sagging leather chair, glass in one hand, cigar in the other, and pronounce his opinion on local politics, the world in general, and which horse was most likely to win the steeplechase at Randwick. Win remained in the background, saying very little, and no-one would have suspected that she took more than a passing interest in Greg Sullivan, an up-and-coming young lawyer who wrote poetry, argued good-humouredly with Ern, and sometimes beat him at chess. Greg was seldom absent whenever I was there, and he seemed to be part of the family.

Of course there were the Deans, the Jenkinses, the Beebys, the Godfreys, the Hilders, the Mortons, the Ken Thomases, and a number of others whose names I cannot recall, but they had a nebulous quality and while, no doubt, they had their troubles and their petty triumphs just the same as I did, I was unaware of them. Perhaps I was the poorer for that lack of interest but they were so secure, so self-righteous, so completely moral that they irritated me. Also, they were bores, and that, in my opinion, was the unforgivable sin. Nevertheless, I did make an effort to be more sociable by joining Louise Lightfoot's class in dancing and eurythmics. We met on Tuesday afternoons in Eric Nicholls's house and waved our arms and swayed and pretended that we were trees in the wind or nymphs in a glade or even birds on the wing, while Louise played suitable music on her zither.

We wore what were still known as bloomers, a sort of pantaloon with elastic round the waist and fastening each leg above the knee. Our feet were bare, and as it was winter and the floors were uncarpeted, our feet got cold. So Molly, Eric's wife, produced several pairs of his woollen socks, which she handed round for us to wear. The sight of half a dozen women solemnly prancing round the room, pretending to be trees with Eric's socks flapping round their feet was too much for Roberta and me, so we disgraced ourselves by rolling about in laughter and were sternly reprimanded by Louise. That was my last appearance in her class.

I might have done better in the drama group, which was rehearsing *Iphigenia in Aulis*. It was shortly to be performed in the rather grandly named New Haven Theatre, which was no more than a ledge of rock on one side of a narrow gully and a semi-circle of roughly hewn stone that served as seats on the other. Nevertheless, some praiseworthy performances of *A Midsummer Night's Dream, As You Like It* and the Greek classics took place there, with Louise Lightfoot's dancing class supplying the necessary chorus. It was lit by acetylene flares, which had a tendency to go out at crucial moments and had to be relit by Bim Hilder, who was adept at climbing over rocks and dodging other hazards in the dark.

Everyone enjoyed themselves, especially the cast, and there would be a party afterwards in someone's house, with claret cup and homemade cakes and sandwiches and congratulations to the cast for having remembered their lines and not fallen down the cliff and to the audience for having endured the swarms of mosquitoes and the discomfort of the seats. I was not given a part in *Iphigenia* because of my pregnancy, but Guido was very much involved. He had been induced to put himself, and his car, at the disposal of the drama group by 'the woman on The Parapet', who was one of its most active members (which was another reason I preferred to be overlooked), and he spent a lot of his time collecting props and bits of scenery and driving Ula to rehearsals in town when I felt he should have been with me. So I did not go to the after-performance party, but went home to bed and felt exceedingly ill used.

The New Haven Theatre went dark soon after that, as its guiding spirit, Marian Griffin, went back to her native Chicago and there was no-one with sufficient enthusiasm to take her place. Soon after Griffin died she had come back from India and spent two years at Castlecrag, and her gaunt, restless figure had become a familiar sight as she strode through the bush and clambered over rocks in a desperate attempt to overcome the sense of desolation that the loss of the man she had adored had brought to her. She rarely spoke of him and once, when she did, it was an eloquent revelation of her grief.

'Waltie has gone away and left me and I never want to hold a pen or a brush in my hand again.'

This, from the woman whose exquisite sketches and watercolour renderings of her husband's designs have a touch of genius and are collectors' items today, can be taken as a measure of her grief. Eric Nicholls, who had been Griffin's partner and was now responsible for his affairs, begged her to remain in Sydney and watch over Castlecrag, but this she resolutely refused to do. One of Eric's first acts on assuming authority was to lift a number of the restrictions on the place imposed by Griffin's covenant, so land was starting to sell and houses that he would never have sanctioned were being built. This must have displeased her very much, and after two years she left.

But she lived for another twenty-five years, and before she died, at the age of ninety-two, she did hold a pen in her hand again and left a record of what had taken place in Canberra, where she and Walter had dreamt of creating a city that would be the envy of the world. Instead of which, they encountered envy and suspicion, calumny and hatred that broke their hearts. She filled twelve volumes, which were thought too incendiary to publish, so they lie hidden in the vaults of the New York Historical Society.

The National Library in Canberra is endeavouring to obtain them, but whether they will ever be published is a matter of some doubt.

Griffin's estate was valued at a pitiful £7 956.1.3d, with debts amounting to £15 026.14.8d. The records say that 'no death duties were imposed'.

CHAPTER 6

After endless delays, the house was finally ready for us to occupy, and in August 1939 we said goodbye to the House of the Seven Lanterns and crossed the road with what few belongings we possessed, among them the bed that had harboured the nasty little bugs in Louisa Road. We had slept side by side on it for over three years, and I had had enough, so, regardless of cost, I went into the classiest furniture store in Sydney, and bought a splendid inner spring on which one seemed to float rather than recline. But even that was not enough to rouse Guido from his lethargy. In short, he had made no attempt to make love to me since, by unspoken agreement, we had ceased to do so during my pregnancy. It did not trouble me then, or in the exhausting postnatal months, but now my libido had returned and I was eager to bring the prolonged chastity to an end. But whatever overtures I made, I met with no response.

This was something new in my experience. Never before had a man remained indifferent to me as Guido did, and I felt rejected and confused.

Ula, the woman on The Parapet, was responsible, of that I was convinced. She had gradually become an accepted factor in my life since the time when I had realised that Guido's interest in her was not solely political. He had insisted that I raise no objection to her then, and I had gradually overcome my prejudice and had learnt to like and even love her. So I was prepared to compromise, to have a *ménage à trois*, if that was the price I had to pay for Guido.

There was also the lingering hope that he would grow tired of her and return to me. If that should be the case, how much better it would be to keep up the pretence that everything was normal, that she and Guido were just good friends. Refusing to have her in the house and generally raising hell was likely to drive Guido out of the house as well.

Then came that September night when Neville Chamberlain's sombre voice came over the radio and informed the world that England was at war with Germany.

I was alone in the house and watched the shadows deepening among the trees and the lights on the opposite shore begin to twinkle in the gloom. 'The lights are going out all over Europe,' Neville Chamberlain had said, and I wondered how long it would be before the lights went out on Sydney Harbour as well.

But, of course, they never did go out. We had what was called a 'brownout': street lights were dimmed, headlights reduced to a glimmer so that we drove through the darkened streets at a crawl; we hung thick curtains over our windows, stood buckets of sand in corridors to put out the fires that never came; and while petrol, clothes and food were rationed, we suffered few deprivations at all, though cigarettes and alcohol were rather scarce until the Americans arrived in 1942.

That was still some way ahead. Meanwhile I had my own problems to think about. My decision to preserve the status quo in my domestic life was badly shaken when I learnt that Ula was suing for divorce. There had always been a husband somewhere in the background but he had been so unobtrusive as to seem nonexistent, and that she should choose to divorce him at that particular time could have only one implication: she intended to marry Guido. This put an end to all my ideas of a *ménage à trois*, and I began to seriously consider the prospect of being by myself.

It filled me with dismay. Never in my life had I led anything but a sheltered existence. There had been my mother, then the man I had married at nineteen, after that the years with Guido when I had felt so totally secure. That security was now about to end. I was in a strange city with few friends, my family had disowned me, and I was exposed to all the hazards that beset a woman with a child and no man to defend her.

There was no child endowment then, no unmarried mother

bounty provided by the government, and no sympathy for a woman who had defied the moral code as blatantly as I had done.

'You have made your bed, my girl, so you must lie in it' my Aunt Belle's voice echoed in my ears.

Inevitably, my thoughts went back to Montsalvat and Justus Jorgensen, the man who had thumbed his nose at public opinion and created a world of his own. Would there be a corner in that world for me?

Several years had passed since the day he had drawn a sketch of his new world in the dust on the hill at Eltham. Then it had seemed like a harmless piece of fantasy, but the buildings had taken shape, he had established a community of devoted followers and he was beholden to no man. The more I thought about it, the more attractive the idea became. But caution warned me to be wary of committing myself. The man was a tyrant who demanded total obedience; I had realised that in those far-off days when I had sat in his studio and listened to monologues about himself, his art, and the place of women in his household. Could I ever submit to his will? Was he less of an autocrat now than he had been then? There was only one way to find out.

Guido had expressed a wish to go down to Melbourne on a number of occasions, as Mike and Neura, now married, were living in 'Larnoo' and were talking of selling the place and going to live somewhere on the Barrier Reef. He still loved the nice old house and wanted to see it before it passed into other hands, so he readily agreed when I said I would like to visit Montsalvat and see how the experiment in communal living was progressing. In addition to 'Larnoo', he had other matters to attend to. He was no longer a member of the Communist Party as the doubts that had tormented him at the time of the trials and execution of the Old Bolsheviks in 1935 had been confirmed in 1939 by the infamous Hitler–Stalin Non-Aggression Pact that cleared the way for the invasion of Poland and the start of World War II. It was a bitter disillusion and had a profound effect on him, but his revolutionary zeal was undiminished and he joined the Trotskyists, a small and rather ineffective opposition to the powerful Stalinists, and badly in need of new recruits. There were a few promising members in Melbourne, and it was Guido's hope of adding to their number that made him so ready to agree that we should visit Jorgensen and Montsalvat. Accordingly, late in January 1941 we boarded the SS *Ormiston*, a sturdy little vessel that, despite the threat of submarines and floating mines, still continued to ply up and down the coast at regular intervals. Two days later we arrived in Melbourne, collected the caravan that we had arranged to hire, attached it to the rear of our car and towed it out to Eltham.

It was late afternoon when we arrived. There was nobody in sight, so we parked in the shade of a tree and took stock of our surroundings. It was an impressive sight. In the four years since we had last been there Jorgensen's dream had been realised to an extent we had not expected. The Gothic great hall was no more than a half-finished shell, but its noble proportions were plainly visible, and the single-storeyed buildings clustered round it gave the impression of a mediaeval village, which was precisely what he had intended.

'I had fallen in love with the Renaissance,' he said, 'and wanted to create an image of it for myself.'

Close beside the future great hall was a charming Tudor cottage with dormer windows, gabled ends and steep slate roof. While we stood admiring it, one of its french doors opened and Jorgensen's wife, Lil, came out. It was a full four years since we had seen her last, and while her smile and the courageous lift to her head were unchanged, she seemed uncertain of her balance and her steps were slow. But her welcome was as warm as ever, and she took us inside and gave us a cup of tea. Max, her son, now eight years old, lay on his stomach on the floor, busily scribbling on some sheets of drawing-paper. He barely looked up when his mother spoke to him and grunted when she urged him to say hello.

'He's a bit shy with strangers, but he'll soon get used to you,' said Lil.

When we had drunk our cup of tea and got up to go, she told us that dinner was served at half past seven each evening and that 'Jorgy' liked people to be punctual. We went back to the caravan and prepared to renew our acquaintance with the Master of Montsalvat—at seven-thirty precisely.

And so began four weeks at Jorgensen's retreat from the modern world. I came away convinced that there was no haven there for me. I had seen arrogance, intolerance, even inhumanity that had astonished me, and marvelled at the docility with which Jorgensen's followers accepted his authority. I had been prepared to accept the discipline and negation of self the Communist Party demanded because it had appeared to represent a great ideal, but Jorgensen appeared to have no ideal greater than the promotion of himself, and to that I could not subscribe.

It was with a heavy heart that I said goodbye and went back to Castlecrag, still uncertain of what I was going to do and what the future held for me.

There were brighter moments among the disillusion of those four weeks, some of them provided by the appearance of two young friends of Guido's, members of the Melbourne Trotsky party, therefore especially prized by him—but not by Jorgensen. They came breezing in one Saturday afternoon without having been invited, a heinous offence in Jorgensen's eyes, and when he observed the flutter they caused among the female members of his community, he ordered them to be shown out the gate.

Saturday nights were gala nights at Montsalvat, as the frugal meals of the week were replaced by what was relatively a banquet and only a chosen few were invited to partake.

'There won't be enough food to go around,' the Master said. 'Tell them if they're hungry they can get a meat pie in the village.'

Two very indignant young men departed villagewards, and whether they bought themselves a meat pie or caught the next train back to Melbourne remains a mystery, but there is no mystery about who they were. One was Laurie Short, the future general secretary of the powerful Ironworkers' Union, the other was destined to become a cabinet minister in the Whitlam government, later the presiding judge of the Land and Environment Court of New South Wales, His Honour Justice James McClelland, 'Diamond Jim' himself.

CHAPTER 7

With Montsalvat ruled out as an alternative to Castlecrag, I now had to find another solution to my problem, the most immediate being how to support myself and my child when there was no longer Guido to depend on. It was time to take stock of my assets, such as they were, and decide how best to utilise them.

I was thirty-seven years of age, but time had been lenient and I could pass for twenty-five. My health was good and my reflection in the mirror not displeasing. Beyond them what else did I have? One good play, *The Touch of Silk*, which had largely been forgotten, two others which had met with no success, and a brief experience in journalism.

I decided on the last, and was taken on as a 'casual' by the *Sydney Evening Sun*, now no longer extant. The editor at the time had eyes so pale and cold and a skin so pallid that he was known as The White Shark. Why he ever took me on, I can't imagine. My first assignment was to write a feature article on the Tanaka Memorial, a document of which I had never heard. A frantic appeal to Guido did not help. He knew all about the Japanese General and his Memorial, which appeared to be a document outlining the strategy that would guarantee victory in the Pacific war. Guido gave me a scant outline of the details. Utterly confused, I sat in front of the typewriter in a state of mental shock and had to admit defeat.

My second ordeal was to be sent to report on a conference being held at the Trades Hall. When I got there at two o'clock I found a deserted room and was told that the conference had ended at half past twelve. I'll swear to this day that I had been told the time was two o'clock.

The White Shark and I were in total accord when I said that I did not feel that I was suited to the job.

That left the doubtful claim to being a successful playwright. On the strength of *The Touch of Silk* and some fifteen-minute plays I had sold to the ABC some years ago, I asked to see Lesley Rees, then drama editor in Sydney. He proved sympathetic and promised me some work, but it would only be at intervals and what I needed was a steady income. So, on his advice, I went to see Mason Wood at radio station 2GB. As it happened, 2GB was urgently in need of scripts for *Dr Mac*, one of the station's evergreen serials, which drew a huge audience all over Australia, so I was given some sample scripts and told to see what I could do.

I came back in a week with five scripts in my hand. Woody looked surprised, glanced at them and laid them on his desk.

'Thank God for someone who can write good dialogue,' were his unforgettable words, and I knew I had a job. The fee per episode was two pounds, and I was to deliver five scripts every week.

The break with Guido came soon after that. Perhaps the weekly pay envelope had something to do with that, but four years of unbroken chastity had strained my endurance to the limit and I felt that it must end. While we were at Montsalvat I had told Lil all about it, and she had taken me to task for letting it go on so long. She was in much the same position as myself, as Jorgensen had fallen in love with one of his young and pretty students and made no secret of the fact, insisting that she raise no objection when the girl came to live with them. He also ceased to share with her the large four-poster bed that they had brought back from Paris. Whether the multiple sclerosis that then afflicted her was the result of that cannot be proven, but that she found consolation in the arms of other men is beyond dispute, and she strongly advised me to do the same. But I had no heart for that. Not yet. I wanted Guido, and no other man would do.

In the five years I had been in Sydney, I had met few men and, apart from Guido's political colleagues, the ones I knew were all living at Castlecrag. Without exception, they were married, and most of them were rather dull. There were men at 2GB, of course, but I had very little contact with them. I went in every Friday afternoon, delivered my quota of *Dr Macs* or whatever else I had written for them, collected my weekly cheque, and then went home again. Furthermore, they were a hard-drinking, chain-smoking lot, each with a gastric ulcer and the inevitable wife, so were no use to me. I might have found someone to my taste on the *Evening Sun* but The White Shark, by assigning me tasks that were far beyond my range, had effectively put an end to that. So unless I broke away from Guido and Castlecrag, it seemed as though I must continue living like a nun.

Lil Jorgensen had told me that it was no use brooding over my hard fate and that, failing to find myself a lover, I must find something else to occupy my mind. Something stimulating and creative, she had said. So I decided to burn up some of my surplus energy by becoming an impresario: in other words, making use of Eric Nicholls's ingenious plan of a circular room that could be transformed into a theatre by merely opening a few doors. Thus the Pangloss Theatre came into existence, 'Pangloss' in memory of the priest in Voltaire's *Candide* who, when things were at their very worst, declared that the world was 'the best of all possible worlds' and one should cultivate one's garden.

I cultivated mine by sponsoring some plays, a string quartet, Louise Lightfoot's dancing class, a young man who spoke about the New Oxford Movement and a three-day seminar organised by the British Drama League one Easter weekend, and was an unqualified success. The final performance was a play by a French author called Simon Gantillon; its title was *Maya* and the action took place in a room in the red light district of Marseilles. This was another unqualified success and might have gone on for weeks had not the Japanese Kamikaze decided to bomb Pearl Harbour on the night of 7 December 1941, and the lights went out on Sydney Harbour and on the Pangloss Theatre as well.

Before Pearl Harbour the war had been an abstraction, something one read about or heard on the evening news; now it was at our door. The fall of Singapore, the lava-like flow through Burma, the Malay States and New Guinea, worst of all the air

47

raids on Darwin and the Western Australian coast, followed in quick succession, and panic replaced complacency, not least on Castlecrag.

The chief concern was the children; where could they be hidden from the menace of the little yellow men?

I remembered a valley hidden deep in the Blue Mountains. Apart from the odd bushwalker—the Duncans had told me about it—few were aware of its existence, but there was a farmhouse there that took in paying guests, and I had spent a holiday there. It was homely and unpretentious, but had a stream flowing past its door and was hemmed in by precipitous cliffs. If it could not promise absolute security, it was at least an improvement on a headland facing Sailors Bay. A meeting of anxious parents was called and I volunteered to drive to the Megalong Valley and discover if the owners of Kirby's farm would agree to let us take over the place until the danger was past. We did not care to think of the alternative.

The Kirbys were more than happy to have us there; their sons had gone to the war and paying guests were scarce. By the end of January the exodus from Castlecrag began.

Word of the plan had got around and we were besieged by other parents who begged us to include their children, but there was a limit of twelve. Ula and her daughter Deirdre were among the fortunate twelve—Ula was a fully trained nurse and would be invaluable should sickness of any kind attack the little refugees. There was a second woman who had formerly taught at school; her husband had been taken prisoner at Singapore and she welcomed the opportunity of finding relief from her anxiety by holding a daily class at Kirby's farm. She had two children, a boy of six and a baby not yet able to walk. There was a little family of three, whose parents were also prisoners of war. They had stayed behind when the Japanese had overrun New Guinea but managed to get their children away in time. They were a forlorn little group, a girl of twelve, a boy of ten and a girl who clung to her sister's skirt and could not control her tears. There had been tears on the part of the other members of the group when it was time to say goodbye, but these soon dried. Home was not far away, and they had promises of weekend visits, letters and telephone calls, and the dust had scarcely settled behind the departing cars before they were splashing in the creek at the bottom of the orchard as though they had come to a picnic.

It was my turn to shed some tears when I left to go back to Sydney the following day. Everyone was at the gate to wave me on my way, Gilda, of course, among them. I looked back as I drove away and noticed how she clung to Ula's hand. No sign of tears from her. She was overjoyed at finding herself no longer an only child; she had suddenly acquired a whole family of boys and girls of her own age, particularly Deirdre. There was already the beginning of a bond between them that was to last for the rest of their lives. Ula she looked upon as a kind of second mother. She had been so often at the house at Castlecrag and seemed so much a part of our lives that I could understand why she had seen me go without a single tear.

Nevertheless, I felt a stab of female jealousy. And reproached myself for doing so. Would I prefer to have had her cling to me and weep as some of the other children had done? No, not that, but I did resent the ease with which she had accepted my absence and attached herself to my rival.

Ula had always roused conflicting emotions in my heart. In spite of all that had happened, I could not really dislike her. She was so generous, warmhearted and unselfish. Had it not been for Guido, I would have loved her. It was a painful position to be in, to both love and dislike someone at the same time, one that must be resolved one way or another. Now seemed to be the time.

Preoccupied with my own thoughts, I did not notice the miles as they slipped past, and I reached Castlecrag in the late afternoon. The house was deserted. Guido had doubtless gone to one of his endless political meetings and there was no-one there to welcome me but Mate. He seemed delighted to see me and fawned around me and licked my face as I bent to pat his head, but as soon as I had fed him his usual pound of gravy beef he disappeared on business of his own. It must be confessed that I indulged myself that night in an orgy of self-pity.

Though I felt Gilda's absence very keenly, it was pleasant to be alone with Guido once again. We could linger over a meal and talk as we used to do without her demanding our attention, and the old close relationship seemed to return. Except for the one essential thing, of course, and as long as that was absent nothing was complete. Otherwise, Guido was affectionate and almost lover-like, which encouraged me to think that, perhaps, he was relieved that Ula was no longer accessible or that his feeling for her had cooled. Should that be the case, I had to know, as my entire future depended on it. As we sat on opposite sides of the table one evening, quietly sipping our wine, I reached out and took his hand.

'Guido, couldn't you please come back to me? I can't go on like this.' He put down his glass and his face lost all expression. 'I love you, Guido, and I need you. What have I done that you don't want me any more?'

'Betsy darling, you've done nothing. Nothing at all.'

'Then, why don't you make love to me?'

He took a long time to reply and when he did, his voice was strained. 'I can't explain.'

There was such a look of sorrow on his face that I said nothing more. I had made my last appeal to him and had got no response. There was no point in going on. It was the end.

In the early stages of the war a certain Dr Norman Haire had returned to Sydney. Thirty years before he had gone off to London having vowed that he would never set foot in the benighted place again, but a well-aimed bomb that demolished his house in Harley Street made him change his mind and he decided that Sydney was a better place to be in than London in its finest hour. Sydney, by and large, was unaware of his existence or of the reputation he had acquired during his years abroad. But he soon changed all that. Contrary to the ethics of the medical profession he saw no reason to be modest or why a little self-promotion was not totally acceptable, so he gave interviews to the press and talks on the ABC which left no-one in any doubt that he was a very distinguished gentleman. He specialised in gynaecology and sexual disorders, and had written a book entitled *The Encyclopedia of Sex*. All of which was enough to make me hurry off and buy it.

It was a very enlightening book indeed, and I learnt much that explained a number of things that had previously been a mystery to me. I came to the conclusion that its author was not such a mountebank as he appeared and was entitled to some respect. This was further confirmed when I read a book by Ethel Mannin, then one of the most successful authors in England. She had fallen under his spell and gave a glowing account of the man in her book of memoirs, *Confessions and Impressions*, which by then had achieved the remarkable total of fifty editions! One particular passage impressed me very much:

> I often wonder what conventional people coming to Norman Haire's house for the first time, without having been previously warned, must think, when they are shown into a consulting-room with a silver ceiling and walls hung with exquisite Chinese embroideries on silk . . . The dining-room is even more exotic, with highly coloured dragons writhing like vorticism-gone-mad all over the ceiling. More silken tapestries here, too, and in the drawing-room, where an almond tree blossoms in paint on the ceiling . . .
>
> Norman Haire would be as remarkable a personality without all that long story of his activities as set forth in *Who's Who*. But there is one very definite aspect of his career which stands out as worthy of comment . . . He came to England from Australia only ten years ago. Nobody in England knew anything about him; in spite of a brilliant medical career in Australia, so far as England was concerned he had done nothing and was nobody; he took a single room in Harley Street and sat down and waited—and hoped. A great many medical men have done that—and finally packed up and gone away. But as a result of Norman Haire's waiting and hoping it is almost

impossible to move about anywhere to-day without his name sooner or later cropping up . . . Everyone, it would seem, either knows Norman Haire—or is hoping to.

It was not long before the same could be said of Sydney, not excluding myself. I had been feeling so badly in need of sound advice, and Ethel Mannin's book had convinced me that Norman Haire was the man to see.

He had taken rooms in Macquarie Street and the first appointment I could get was three weeks ahead. It certainly paid to advertise.

Ethel Mannin had led me to expect a man of enormous charm, genial and handsome, in short, a woman's dream of what a man should be, but the reality failed to fulfil the dream. Instead of the golden-haired Adonis I had hoped to see, here was a corpulent, rather pompous-looking individual in late middle age, with a florid face and thatch of reddish hair around his balding pate. Nor was that the only surprise. Prominently displayed on the table in his consulting room was a notice that said: 'Patients are requested to settle their accounts at the conclusion of the consultation', something so unheard of in those days as to be even more outrageous than self-promotion. But there was worse to come.

After asking for the necessary details such as how old I was, how many children I had, how often I menstruated, he delivered the ultimate shock by asking how often did I masturbate! At the sight of my startled face he hastened to reassure me by saying that he asked the same question of all his patients and that, if they denied ever having been guilty of such an unspeakable act, he informed them that they were either untruthful or abnormal. Thus encouraged, I assured him of my normality. After that, it was easy to tell him about my problems with Guido.

'Do you realise he's given you grounds for divorce?' he asked.

'I can't divorce him, because I'm not married to him.'

His expression seemed to change at that, as though I had emerged from the grey mass of ordinary people and become an individual. We got on very well after that.

'I don't know what you're worrying about,' he said at last. 'You're a young and healthy woman. Why don't you get yourself another man? You should have no difficulty. Sydney's alive with young, sex-hungry men.'

'You mean, soldiers?'

'Yes. You'd be doing them a favour and saving yourself from becoming neurotic. You're on the way to that already.'

'Am I?'

'Yes. Look at the way you're fiddling with your purse.'

How many years was it since the same thing had been said to me? It was during another crisis in my life. The time when I had first learnt that Peter, my little son, would die when he was seven. My anguish had been the same and I had found release from the pain by a series of sexual excesses with men for whom I felt no love. Perhaps I should try the same therapy again.

With these thoughts in my mind it was natural that I should be unaware of the man who paused beside my table as I ate my lunch and asked did I mind if he joined me. I looked up and saw a man in uniform, a tall, good-looking man who seemed about thirty years of age. I told him he could sit in the vacant chair and took no further notice of him. But he was not to be deterred. He told me later that he had seen me sitting there alone, and liked the look of me, and decided he would try to get to know me. It seemed more than a coincidence that a man like Edward Powell should walk into a restaurant like the Monterey, which was rather second-class, and obey an instinct that was so foreign to his nature. But he was also strange to Sydney, had spent his life in the western part of New South Wales, it was his first week in the army, his first day of leave, and he was very lonely. All this I learned as the afternoon progressed.

We talked until the waitress grew impatient and slammed the bill on the table as a hint that it was time for us to go. After that we spent the remainder of the afternoon in Hyde Park, still talking, and I learnt that he was married and had a little daughter that he adored, and I told him about Guido, giving no details though, and about Gilda and Megalong and that I was

53

not happy. The sun began to set and we walked to the Quay and got on a Manly ferry. The brownout was strictly observed and all the lights were dim along the Corso, while along the Esplanade no lights shone at all. The unlit buildings had a ghostly appearance and there was no-one but ourselves, apart from the sentries on duty who watched us as we passed and murmured a goodnight. There were barbed-wire entanglements everywhere and gun emplacements on the headland. We paused in the shadow of one of these and he kissed me, very tenderly, and asked me would I meet him again next day and spend the night with him. I said I would and then went back to Castlecrag.

Guido was already in bed when I got home. He asked me where I had been and what I had done. I told him everything and what I had promised to do. He did not seem disturbed.

'Is he an American?'

'No, Australian.'

'Is he a decent sort of chap?'

'I think so.'

'Good. I'm glad of that.'

The lack of emotion chilled me. He was so indifferent that he did not care. I got into bed and he put out the light.

Next afternoon when it was time for me to go, he was busy in his study and put down his pen when he saw me at the door.

'It's time for me to go,' I said and he glanced at his watch.

'Yes, I suppose it is.' Still no protest, no effort to persuade me not to keep my appointment. Slowly, sadly, I walked up the hill. Near the bus stop there was a public telephone. I dialled the number, still unable to believe that he could let me go without a word of protest.

'Guido, do you understand that I am going to spend the night with this man? The *night*.' I had to be quite sure.

'Yes, Betsy, I understand.'

There was nothing more to be said, so I caught the bus and met my soldier as arranged.

I had said he was a 'nice bloke' and I was not wrong. I think I could have loved him, but there were the wife and child in

Dubbo whom neither of us could forget. He was sent to the officer's training school at Duntroon, commissioned and then posted to New Guinea. We met a few times before he went and then I lost touch with him; he did not write and I had not expected him to. Then for some reason I cannot explain, I went to the Monterey again. Perhaps I was missing him, I do not know, but he was certainly in my thoughts, and when I looked up and saw him standing before me, for a moment I thought that I was seeing a ghost. He was as astonished as I was, as he had also acted on a sudden whim to revisit the Monterey, not in the hope of seeing me but because he had happy recollections of the place. He was also depressed and lonely, as he had been badly wounded in New Guinea and was shortly to be invalided out of the army and would return to Dubbo.

I took him back to Castlecrag with me. I was living there alone, as Guido and I had agreed to part the year before. It was a flawless night. The moon was so bright we needed no other light as we sat on the terrace and ate our simple meal and drank our wine. Afterwards, when my hands strayed on his naked back, I felt the small round scar which the bullet made when it pierced his lung; there was another scar on his chest where it had entered. Later, as we walked together up the hill, I could hear his laboured breathing; once he staggered a little and we paused to let him rest. That bullet had done more damage than the small round wounds had indicated.

We said goodbye at the corner of Edinburgh Road, and that was the last I ever saw of him. I could have loved him very dearly, and I have no doubt that he was in love with me, but there were the wife and child at home in Dubbo and he had pledged himself to them. So I returned to the empty house and he became a memory.

CHAPTER 8

Brief though it was, the encounter with Edward Powell was the catalyst that brought about the final break with Guido. Shortly after that first night at the Metropole Hotel he announced his intention of paying a few days' visit to Kirby's farm. This was no surprise, as he had already done so on a couple of occasions, and I watched him go with no premonition of what would be the result. So when he said on his return that there was something that he wanted to discuss with me, I was unprepared for the revelations he was about to make. His voice had a portentous ring and he looked a little grim, and I assumed that he was going to take me to task for something I had done.

'I want you to know that I slept with Ula while I was at Megalong,' he began and paused to see what my reaction would be.

I showed no surprise. 'Is that something new?'

'Yes, it is.'

I stared in disbelief. 'You mean to say that you haven't been sleeping with her all this time?'

'No, I haven't.'

'You can't be serious! I don't believe you!'

'Nevertheless, it's true.'

'You've kept us both on the hook!' Anger was starting to rise. 'What's the matter with you, Guido? Why have you done this to both of us?'

'I was waiting until you were ready.'

'Ready for what?'

'To be left alone.'

'Does that mean you want to go and live with her?'

'Yes, someday I do.'

'Someday! What are you waiting for? Why not now?'

'That's for you to say.'

'Then I'll say it. Go *now*. Get out of my life and give me a chance to find someone else.' Hasty, ill-considered words, which I was often to regret, but all I could feel was anger, that somehow I had been made a fool of. That he had gone to bed with Ula in order to get even with me. How else to explain the fact that this act of infidelity had so soon followed mine? I was not thinking very clearly and allowed my emotions to run away with me.

'I want Gilda,' I said. 'I want her back immediately. I'm going to Megalong to get her.'

'Just as you wish.'

This maddening compliance. If only he had protested when I told him I was going to spend the night with Edward Powell, how easily I could have been induced to change my mind. And now, if he had tried to reason with me when I told him he must go, I might have taken back my words. But he said nothing and I drove off to Megalong, bitterness and anger raging in my heart.

When I came back next day, he had already packed his things. It was another shock to see how readily he was prepared to go, and effectively dried up any appeal I might have made to him to stay. So I drove him into the city and left him on the footpath outside Pharlett's Hotel, where Ula had already agreed to meet him, and then went back to Castlecrag to begin a new life alone.

The pain did not begin for several days. There was a period of feverish excitement. I could not stay still, I could not settle to anything, not even *Dr Mac*. I went to a party at the Heslings' place. A rather artificial crowd was there, among them a man called Hal Missingham who sang bawdy songs which everyone enjoyed except myself. I hated all of them, especially pretty Flo who seemed more self-satisfied than usual, and the ever-pregnant cat whose sagging belly seemed obscene. Bernard did his improvisation of a Handel oratorio. I had heard it several times before and had thought it was hilarious but this time thought how ridiculous he looked with his bald head, receding chin and protruding teeth.

Then someone asked me why Guido was not there.

'Didn't you know he's left me? Gone to live with someone else,' I said, taking a perverse delight in their astonished look. It was the same when I met Harold Morton's wife the following day.

'Not again,' she said when I mentioned Ula's name. I wondered what she meant but did not bother to ask.

Then necessity drove me back to the typewriter, and some of the tension eased. But that did not help me at night. It was then that the daemons crept out of the shadows and gibbered at me. What were Guido and Ula doing? Was he making love to her? Was he saying the tender, silly things that he had once said to me? Why had I not turned her out of the house when I first began to suspect that she was trying to take him away from me? In that way I would generate a seething volcano of hatred which would erupt in tears and send me to bed to toss restlessly for hours.

It was no help when Guido came out to see me. He was anxious about me and noticed the lines of strain on my face. He would hold my hand and murmur soothing words and be so tender and sympathetic that when he had gone away I would shed floods of tears and yearn for him as though he had never behaved in the dastardly way he had. In its way, his concern was a refined form of cruelty; it prevented me from forgetting, and kept me in love with him.

Unlike Karen Blixen, whose book *Out of Africa* I both envy and admire, there has been little in the way of poetry in my emotional life. Guido and the brief encounter with Edward Powell are the exceptions, but otherwise it has been ill-advised, painful and even crude; an example of which was the affair with the man I shall refer to as Nick.

Not long after I left Guido standing outside Pharlett's Hotel in Margaret Street a convoy of army trucks had come grinding down the hill at Castlecrag, shattering the silence and scaring away the birds. The men on board belonged to a transport unit of the AIF that had been evacuated from Ingleburn and ordered to set up camp in the less conspicuous picnic ground below my

59

house. Which they proceeded to do, rousing my indignation by cutting down some of Burley Griffin's beloved trees and lighting fires where none had been permitted to burn before. I was further annoyed by their loud voices, raucous songs, and wolf whistles whenever they caught sight of me as they drove past.

Then the monsoon arrived. The rain poured down in torrents, cascading down the road and turning the picnic ground into a morass. I began to feel guilty because I had a warm bed to sleep in while the men in B Company had canvas stretchers and sodden blankets and had trouble in keeping their fires alight. So I sent word to say they could come and bivouac in the empty rooms in the house until the rain dried up. That is how it began.

Nick was different to the others. He was sullen and inclined to grumble while the others were invariably cheerful and full of jokes. I found him attractive; I liked the way he sat in the background and made no attempt to join them in their games and horseplay. Especially I liked the way he looked at me. His eyes were very dark, almost black, which made me wonder if he had native blood in his veins. They followed me around the room in a watchful, speculative way as though he was weighing up my possibilities—in bed. It was not long before he found out.

I did not have to invite him, he just came in one night when I was already in bed, threw the bedclothes back and made love to me in a way that I had not even dreamt about before. We scarcely spoke, but there was one occasion when he said: 'Take it easy. I know you're hungry but it comes better if you wait.' I felt I had been waiting all my life for a man like Nick. He roused a degree of passion in me that I did not know I possessed. In a subtle way he seemed to sense the presence of the hidden secret desires that my body had suppressed and when the ultimate moment came it was both ecstasy and agony, leaving me exhausted and at peace.

Our affair came to an end quite suddenly as the tide of the war turned and the Japs were in retreat, so the men of the AIF were needed in the north and B Company were ordered to take down their tents and proceed to a destination not yet revealed.

The trucks ground past the house for the last time on an early morning in June.

I was like an alcoholic suddenly deprived of drink, I literally craved Nick. I had no idea where he was or when I would see him again and longed for a letter that would stifle my growing doubts. No letter came. Day after day I searched the letter box, hoped that the telephone would ring, like any besotted, love-sick girl. I started to feel resentful and ashamed. I had condescended to him, granted him the privilege of my bed, and he had gone off without a word. So I began a new affair. He was young and inexperienced and I took a perverse delight in teaching him the subtleties that I had learnt from Nick. This had a shattering effect on him. He fell violently in love with me, which was the last thing that I wanted and I soon got bored.

He began to talk of marriage—after the war, of course— and begged me to promise to be faithful to him while he was away. I let him babble on and promised that I would, inwardly thinking that I might never be called to account as he might not return. Let him be happy while he's here, I thought, and was particularly tender to him that night.

Rumours began to circulate that his unit was soon to be sent to the front and he pleaded to be allowed to spend the last days of his pre-embarkation leave with me. It seemed a small thing to do and I agreed. He telephoned one morning to say the time had come and that he would be with me that afternoon. It will soon be over, I told myself, and resolved to make those last two days as memorable as lay within my power.

I planned the perfect dinner and was busy in the kitchen when I heard the sound of footsteps in the inner room. I had not expected him so soon and called to him. There was no answer and I wondered why that was. Drying my hands, I went to see if anything was wrong and there, standing in the middle of the room, was Nick, hat on the side of his head in the usual way, the usual half-mocking expression on his face.

I had to make a choice. I had either to tell Nick to go away or meet that poor deluded boy at the door and tell him the brutal truth. If there is such a thing as a recording angel, which I doubt, I hope he gives me credit for the choice I made. Nick took it well, at least he made no comment when I told him he must go, and why.

'Why didn't you tell me you were coming? Why did you never write?' I asked as he turned towards the door. He stopped and looked back at me.

'Because I was ashamed to let you see I couldn't spell. I'm illiterate, didn't you know?'

There was time to pull myself together before the boy arrived and I was able to give him the welcome he had hoped for. He was in full combat kit: camouflage uniform, tin hat slung on one shoulder, bandoleer across his chest, rifle, water bottle, jungle boots, all of which made him look a bit ridiculous, and at the same time rather sad.

'Does it make me look like a soldier?' he asked. 'I'm damned if I feel like one.'

He looked like the troubled boy he was and I felt a great compassion for him and took him in my arms.

Forty-eight hours soon passed. There was the final long embrace, the few choked words, and then he turned his face away and went up the hill. I closed the door and was thankful that the ordeal was over. But it was not over, not by any means. He did not go back to Ingleburn that day, did not report to his unit, he lost his nerve, went to his parents' home, took off his uniform and became a technical deserter. At some stage during the night he came out to Castlecrag. Nobody slept with bolted doors and windows then, so it was easy for him to get in without disturbing me. I woke quite early, got up to make some coffee and saw him lying on a bed in the spare room.

I thought there had been a change of plan in the embarkation date, but felt a twinge of alarm when I saw he was not in uniform. I asked him what had happened and he blurted out the truth.

'I lost my nerve. It was the thought of leaving you. Darling, I love you so, please say you understand.'

It was then that the ugly side of my nature revealed itself.

I shook free of the clinging hands, raved at him and told him the bitter truth. That I did not love him, never had done, and despised him.

'Get out of here,' I said. 'Go back and get into your uniform and try to behave like a man.'

'It's no use. I can't go back.'

'Why not?'

'Because the others have gone. The transport left at six o'clock this morning. Help me, tell me what I'm to do.'

I had learnt enough of military law from Nick to be able to tell him that if he went back to Ingleburn that day, said he had got drunk and overslept, he would not be charged with desertion, only absence without leave. Wearily, he got up, put on his shabby jacket and prepared to go.

'I don't suppose they'll shoot me,' was his last remark.

They didn't. He was classed as unsuitable for active service and sent to load cargo on the Townsville wharf for the remainder of the war.

The mental anguish of the next few days is something I prefer to forget. With the highest of intentions, I had sent Nick away rather than hurt the boy, and had only succeeded in depriving myself and dealing him a wound that would fester and be slow to heal. I thought of going in search of Nick in the hope of getting him back, but did not know where to look. He was very cagey about his whereabouts when he was not in camp and beyond hinting at friends he had in Woolloomooloo, gave no further details. But he had said something about a woman much older than himself who had picked him up off the street when he was a kid and was a sort of mother to him. Well, not exactly. From the few hints he dropped I guessed the sort of woman that she was.

'She taught me my manners in bed,' he said in one of our most intimate moments. 'Maybe she should teach you a trick or two.' That had made me mad and I had pummelled his chest with my fists.

Sometimes a postcard arrived from one of the men in B

Company. They were now in the jungles of New Guinea and wrote about trivial things, never about the discomforts, the heat, the mud, the tropical ulcers. One of them mentioned Nick.

'You'll be surprised to know that Nick got married when he was on leave to a woman he'd known for a long time. Hasn't improved his temper though, he's as surly as ever.'

This did not hit me as hard as it would have done if I had known at the time, but several weeks had passed and I had begun to realise that, painful though the time had been, I had had a lucky escape. If Nick had asked me to marry him, I would have done so—with disastrous results. Maybe fate had sent the boy to save me from my folly. Lucky for me, but a bit hard on the boy!

CHAPTER 9

While the delirium of those winter months had lasted I had seen very little of my neighbours. A good deal of gossip had been exchanged between them—Roberta had kept me informed of this—and even Guido disapproved of my involvement with the men of B Company.

'What do you think you're doing, behaving like Messalina and the Pretorian Guard?' he said on one occasion, which I thought a shade extreme. But he ceased to visit me so often, which was a good thing.

Roberta, of course, was totally on my side. She used to join the fun on Saturday nights and dance with the boys, and how many of them went home with her was no concern of mine.

It was now four years since I had seen her come so gaily down the hill and she had admired Gilda and said that she must have a baby girl. Nicky, the boy who had come instead, was now three years old and she was no longer the contented wife that she had been. She had put on weight and sometimes drank a bit too much, but had lost none of her former charm. Edgar still doted on her and when, on occasion, she went into town and did not return for a night or two, he would put Nicky into bed, rub Michael's chest with Vicks, and say very little when she got back. Even when she fell in love with an overweight Australian called Franz, he seemed prepared to overlook it. When she fell pregnant and did not have an abortion, he finally rebelled and left. But he soon came back again.

'I was more miserable away from her than I was when I was with her,' he explained in one rare moment of self-revelation. The baby was a girl and he accepted her as well.

'She is Roberta's child as well as his,' he said. Nevertheless, it was Nicky on whom he showered his love. They would go off for the day together, Nicky perched on the front of his bicycle, or astride his shoulders when they went bushwalking with Frank and Anise Duncan, while Michael was left to amuse himself by dressing up in some of Roberta's clothes and dreaming of becoming a ballet-dancer or a film star.

I had felt no wish to get friendly with the Duncans. Frank was a taciturn man who barely noticed me if we happened to meet on the road, and Anise was too meek and colourless to interest me. So it was a surprise when she came to the door one day in obvious distress. Tears were pouring down her face and she was scarcely able to speak.

'It's Ross,' she said when I had led her inside. 'It's his leg. You know the way he has said that it ached. The doctor says it isn't rheumatism as we thought but osteomyelitis. He'll die unless they amputate.'

There were no words with which to offer comfort to the poor distracted mother and I did not try to stop her when she got up to go. I watched her walk away, moaning softly to herself and wringing her hands.

Back in their cute little Burley Griffin house she and Frank had to make their terrible decision: certain death or the surgeon's knife, and even that was no guarantee of recovery. They made the choice that any normal parents would, and the sight of a wan-faced boy on crutches, picking his way painfully along the bush tracks near his home, began to haunt us all. But not for long, and the Duncans were left with Barry, the second son, who had never been so favoured as his brother.

Barry was a quiet little boy who became Gilda's special friend. They had been born within a few days of each other and were inseparable. She tyrannised over him, which he did not seem to mind, and I remember her informing me that she was going to marry him one day.

Castlecrag was scandalised again when Win Claridge created a sensation by leaving Ern to marry the promising young barrister who had spent so many weekends with them. She had seemed so prim, so utterly devoid of warmth that nobody suspected the fire that simmered underneath the chilly exterior. Certainly not

Ern. He was left in a state of near-collapse, and would come to me for sympathy and sit with the tears running down his cheeks, the picture of human misery. I knew exactly how he felt but it was beyond my power to help and I was relieved when his wounds began to heal and he went on fishing trips and to the races at Randwick again. He also brought his old father out to Castlecrag to live with him, giving him someone to play chess with again. Later on, Ern married an old friend and surprised himself by fathering a nine pound baby girl.

After that, Castlecrag resumed the even tempo of its days. My days were fully occupied with writing radio scripts, not only for *Dr Mac* but what would now be called soap operas for other stations, chiefly the George Edwards-Nell Stirling Company, which turned out an astonishing number of serials and gave me a lot of work. And there was Lesley Rees of the ABC, who had not forgotten his promise to commission a play from time to time. These were an oasis in the arid waste of the soap operas of which I was inwardly ashamed, but for which I was happy to receive the rewards of the weekly cheque.

It was about this time that an unexpected piece of good fortune came my way. My disapproving Aunt Belle, who had dealt so harshly with me when we met in London, died, and to my surprise included me among her heirs. It was a seventh share in a considerable estate that was to be held in trust until the last of the original beneficiaries had died, after which the capital was to be equally divided among their children. I was the sole exception. When I died, Gilda would not receive my seventh share, it would go back into the corpus and be divided equally among the survivors.

'No child of Baracchi's shall have any money of mine,' the bitter old woman had said, 'but I'll leave her mother enough to keep her out of the gutter.'

It saddened me to think that poor Gilda should be penalised because of my misdeeds. The income, however, was mine for as long as I stayed alive. I resolved to live forever and amass as much money as I could. Even Aunt Belle could not deprive

Gilda of that. But the income, small though it was at the time, was a godsend.

'You'll be able to take risks,' said Lesley Rees when I told him about it.

Les would have liked to take risks too, but his wife was about to have their first child and he was temporarily anchored to his chair in the ABC. I think of Coralie and Lesley Rees with affection. Not only did Les put work my way, but they were also among the very few people who showed any sign of friendship in that bleak time of my life. Apart from the Heslings, nobody at Castlecrag showed any interest in me at all, much less concern about how I was coping with my solitary state. There was Roberta, of course, but little in the way of comfort could be found with her, and the rest were merely passing acquaintances. No doubt they disapproved of me. But Les and Coralie took me into their house and into their hearts and helped restore a little of my self-esteem. *Gracias!*

I had now progressed beyond *Dr Mac* and was writing serials for other radio stations, but the uncertainty still remained—I never knew where the next pay envelope was coming from. On a number of occasions I thought that I had security within my grasp. Les Rees rang me up one day and asked if I would be interested in writing what he called a 'tea-time' serial which would be broadcast in mid-afternoon. I said that I would be delighted to and wrote the first twenty episodes of *Number Twenty-five* which duly went to air and seemed to be going well. Then Les rang me up again. There had been a reshuffling of programmes, he said, and a choice had been made between *Blue Hills* and *Number Twenty-five*. *Blue Hills* had won, and I was on the freelance list again.

Then Bernard Hesling advised me to go and see the number one man at the J. Walter Thompson Advertising Agency. He was a neat little man with a small moustache, who surveyed me gravely from behind a massive desk.

'It isn't a matter of taking you on to write for us,' he said. 'We have a number of projects under consideration at the present time; it's a case of deciding where best to slot you in.'

I came away feeling that fortune had finally smiled on me, but a letter came informing me that after further consideration, he had reluctantly decided that he could offer me no contract at the present time.

I showed the letter to Bernard, who enquired whether I had been asked the date and place of my birth. I said that I had. 'That explains it,' Bernard said. 'The man's fanatical about astrology. He won't give anyone a job without casting their horoscope. He bets on the races and buys shares on the stock exchange after consulting the stars. Yours must have been awfully bad.' They must indeed, as the next few years were among the blackest in my life.

My stars appeared to have relented somewhat when I went to see George Edwards of the George Edwards–Nell Stirling Production Company sometime afterwards. Sumner Locke Elliott had told me there might be a good job there for me, as the war had depleted their staff of regular writers, himself included. He had just received his call-up papers and was soon to be in uniform.

The George Edwards–Nell Stirling Company was a husband and wife team that were unique. They poured out a stream of well-directed, well-scripted, well-acted serials that had earned them a name for excellence; they were also known to be extremely pleasant to work for, and to be a member of their team of writers was like being a member of a family. So Sumner had informed me. I wanted that job very much and, when the time for the initial interview arrived, made myself look as presentable as possible, firmly believing that first impressions count. The impression that I made on George Edwards was rather different from what I had expected.

He, too, sat at a massive desk, but the room had an opulence that had been missing at the J. Walter Thompson interview. Not missing were the Havana cigar, the reek of VSOP brandy, the flushed face and the air of geniality, danger signals I soon recognised. He suggested that it would be better if I sat beside him instead of on the opposite side of the desk, but I said I was quite happy where I was—tactfully of course—and he gave me a close look as though assessing my reason for doing so. After that, things proceeded as usual. He asked me about the work I had done for other stations, the plays I had adapted for the ABC—he seemed particularly interested in these—finally suggesting that I should demonstrate my skill by adapting the first three chapters of a novel by Georgette Heyer, of which he already had the rights.

All had gone well, and I got up to go. He too got up, as though to open the door, instead of which he managed to manoeuvre me so that I was pinned in the corner of the room with his belly pushed hard against my pubic bone. He stayed that way for a short time, breathing heavily, waiting for my next move. When I stayed absolutely still, showing no emotion, he drew back in disgust.

'God, you're a cold woman,' he said.

The George Edwards-Nell Stirling Company had its city office in the State Theatre building and I can remember standing outside in Market Street, Georgette Heyer's novel clutched in my hand, and thinking: 'What am I going to do? I *must* have that job!'

I went home and rang Sumner to tell him what had happened. He was astounded and doubted my word at first. When I had convinced him that I was telling the truth, he said, 'Well, all I can say is this: if Nell gets wind of it, you're through.' Which did not encourage me in the least. But, sceptic though I was, I felt that Jupiter the beneficent was watching over me that night as, on his way home to Darling Point, George Edwards drove into the back of a tram and was taken off to hospital with concussion and several broken ribs. I read about it next morning in the paper and gave thanks to whatever gods there be. By the time he had recovered I was firmly established with Nell, his wife, and I continued to write serials for the company for several years.

With Aunt Belle's legacy to supplement my earnings I was then in a position every ardent feminist would envy. I had a house, a child, and a steady income with which to maintain them both. Above all, I was free and answerable to no-one. But I felt no sense of jubilation, on the contrary, I was utterly miserable and envied the women who were married and had a man who came home to them at night, who loved them and made love to them and bullied them at times, which was the natural order of things and much to be preferred to my solitary state. Luckily, I had no intimation that this would be my condition for the remainder of my life. On the contrary, I did not doubt that I would have no difficulty in finding someone to take Guido's place. In what way was I different to the woman who could take her pick of half a dozen men before he ever came into my life? For one thing I was ten years older, a decisive factor that I neglected to take into consideration. I was also badly disillusioned, and distrusted the entire male sex, so was considerably handicapped before I even began my search.

It was essential to get away from Castlecrag, that much was clear. But there was Gilda to be considered. She was old enough to go to school and there was no school closer than Willoughby, which meant she had to go by bus as I no longer had a car to take her. She was not yet five years old and that was far too young to manage the journey by herself. I had made up my mind that Kings Cross was the place in which I intended to live and that did not seem to be a good place for her. Then Ula provided a solution that seemed ideal.

She had a friend who lived in Warrawee, on the sedate North Shore whose daughter, Louana, was a little older than Gilda. Louana already went to a nearby school and so would be a kind of elder sister to Gilda during those alarming early days at kindergarten. That is, if Mrs Chapman agreed to have her come and stay with her. Mrs Chapman did, and that meant one of my problems was solved. But only one. I had to find a tenant for the house, and what was even more important, find myself a flat in the overcrowded Cross.

Kings Cross, with its noise, uneasy crowds, its cheap cafes, beggars, touts and tattered women lurking in the doorways, has always held a strong attraction for me from the first day I had seen it. The Cross was where Guido and I had stayed when we

71

first came to Sydney; it was where Gilda had been conceived, and where I would now begin a new life and forget the old. But the Americans had inundated Sydney and the Cross was their favourite haunt, so there wasn't a flat or a room or a hotel bed that was unoccupied in the whole square mile and my chance of finding a place in which to start my life again seemed remote.

But whatever misfortunes may have befallen me, I have always managed to find a pleasant place to live, even in such an unlikely place as Moscow, where I had been saved from a vermin-infested room on the fringes of the city by the fortunate chance that a friend was due to go on leave to England and offered me her flat. By the time she had returned I was due to go to Leningrad, where the shortage was not so acute, and I had been given a room in a brand new building so recently completed that the ubiquitous bedbugs had not had time to move in.

My luck held good in Sydney. I saw an advertisement in the morning paper, hurried to the address and, to my amazement, there was no queue outside the door and the rent was within my means. I could scarcely believe my luck and it shows the wisdom of never failing to read the daily paper, even the advertisements. I had already found a tenant for the house, but before handing over the keys and moving out, a final distressing event took place.

Early in the year Alan Marshall and his wife had spent a few days with me as they passed through Sydney on their way to Queensland. Alan was going in search of material for his book *These Are My Tribesmen*, and Olive, despite the fact that she was three months pregnant, was going with him for as long as her condition allowed. It was not very long, and she soon returned to Melbourne, leaving Alan to pursue his search alone. I was in the throes of packing up when he unexpectedly appeared. I was delighted to see him and listened eagerly to his account of the weeks spent with the people of Arnhem Land, how they had accepted him into their tribe and even allowed him to witness their most secret ceremonies.

Still troubled by the memory of Nick and the fair-haired boy,

I told him what had happened, knowing he would understand and not condemn. He listened with growing concern on his face, and said it was not love that I had felt for Nick, but a thing of the flesh and not of the spirit, and that my present troubled mood would pass. I was not convinced but lay awake that night while he put up his camp-bed in what had been Guido's study and, presumably, went to sleep.

I must have dozed off because I was disturbed by the sound of his crutches padding across the floor of the big room, the circular room, between us. I listened and a sudden suspicion that he was coming to my room shot through me. It couldn't be, I told myself, it was impossible! But the sound continued, and he came through the door. Neither of us spoke. He drew back the bedclothes and eased himself beside me, while I lay in frozen silence, stunned by the knowledge that the impossible had happened.

I have a deep-seated aversion to physical deformity of any kind. I know it to be reprehensible on my part and reproach myself for being that way, but I cannot bear to look at the twisted limbs and distorted bodies of the handicapped. I have to avert my eyes, and feel ashamed at doing so. And here was this man of whom I was so fond, whom I respected for his gifts as a writer and his undefeated courage, but whose body was a mockery of all that the human body should be. If I rejected him it would tell him that I found him repulsive, if I acquiesced it would be with shrinking flesh, and how could I inflict another wound on this courageous being who had had to endure so much?

As I ran my hands along that poor distorted back and felt the twisted spine, I wept inwardly, not solely for Alan but for myself as well.

He left quite soon after breakfast the following morning. Neither of us alluded in any way to what had happened in the night, but it had cost me a friend. He was always elusive after that and seemed to avoid my eyes, which made me very sad.

CHAPTER 10

Opinions are sharply divided about Kings Cross. It is looked upon as either a modern Gomorrah or a source of endless interest and variety. I belong to the latter category. The place had cast its spell over me when, newly come from Melbourne, I had walked with Guido down that unique half-mile that lies between the top of William Street and the Fountain of El Alamein. Neither the litter on the street, the pornographic shops, the touts and pimps, or the scrofulous old deadbeats with their bottles of cheap wine in any way offended me. On the contrary, I found them all immensely interesting—and still do—so it was inevitable that I should choose the Cross as the place in which to exercise my right as a fully liberated woman. The fact that Guido and Ula were living in Darlinghurst Road may have had something to do with it, and I was glad of their proximity as, contrary to my expectations, I was just as lonely in the Cross as I had been at Castlecrag.

As Norman Haire had said, the place was swarming with men, but the majority were Americans and they, I soon discovered, were only interested in the youngest and least intellectual members of the female sex. I marvelled to see them sitting in the most expensive restaurants, orchids cascading down their bosoms, not knowing which fork or spoon to pick up first, totally overwhelmed by the visitation of these god-like creatures from another world. Of course, I envied them; most women of my age shared my feelings. We wanted the attention, nylon stockings, good manners, good looks and tailored uniforms of Uncle Sam's brave boys who had swept into Sydney like an army of conquerors and claimed the spoils of war.

Roberta had a friend called Julia. She was an attractive blonde who did voluntary work in the American canteen in Elizabeth

Street and it was at her suggestion that I also offered my services there two nights a week. It was an amusing sight to see those rows of happy warriors busily sucking Coca-Cola through a straw. The blissful expression on their faces reminded me of babies sucking at a comforter, or maybe it was the maternal tit. The American canteen had its Australian counterpart in Darlinghurst Road and I also donned an apron there and served roast meat and three veg to the taciturn men of the AIF and decided that if it was a choice between the Yanks with their hamburgers, eggs over or sunny-side-up, and the laconic Aussies to stand between me and the Japs, the roast beef and three veg men would win. But I was, no doubt, in a sour frame of mind.

This mood was somewhat lightened by the arrival of Jim McClelland, the brash young man who, along with Laurie Short, had been so unceremoniously shown out the gates of Montsalvat. I had scarcely given him a thought since then. Now he had reappeared in Sydney, no longer a member of the Trotsky Party but a member of the RAAF, and had risen to the rank of Leading Aircraftsman in that privileged elite. He was a reluctant hero as, being both politically and intellectually opposed to war, he had done his best to evade the general call-up and very much resented the fact that he was now in the airforce and must do as he was told.

Guido was one of the few people that he knew in Sydney, so it was inevitable that he should come to see him and that we should meet. It was also inevitable that, in a very short time, he should become my lover.

Jim looked very handsome in his neat blue uniform and was an escort any woman would be happy to be seen with, but his airforce pay did not allow any dinners in expensive restaurants, much less sprays of orchids, so he came and shared a home-cooked meal with me. He also shared my bed and came within an ace of having me evicted from my flat. The landlady was a sour old dame who did not approve of overnight visitors, but the crisis was averted when Jim was posted away to Darwin.

Meanwhile, he continued to spend his free time with me. He

was stationed at Windsor, where he was undergoing a crash course in the mysteries of the newly discovered radar, for which he expressed some disdain. Having mastered that he was sent up north to watch for any Japanese invaders who might take it into their heads to make another raid on the vulnerable north coast. We said goodbye without much regret on either of our parts. I liked him, I admired his keen brain, but he had lit no fire in my heart, nor had I in his.

Perhaps I had been at fault by being too readily accessible, but he was there, I was lonely and aware that the airforce would take him away without warning. That much I had learnt through Nick. There were other things that I had learnt from Nick but had felt no urge to pass that knowledge on to Jim. While I was at Montsalvat, Justus Jorgensen had said that a woman's body was like a violin which in the hands of a skilled musician would vibrate and throb and make beautiful sounds, but in the hands of an amateur would only make screeches and squawks. I don't think I made screeches and squawks, but Jim was no virtuouso either.

So he had come and gone and things were no better with me than they had been before. Kings Cross still pulsed with life, there was the sound of music, the laughter, the lovers walking hand-in-hand or locked in an embrace. How refreshingly uninhibited those Americans were! I wished that one of them would pay some attention to me. But none of them did, and while I did make a few contacts among the men in the canteen in Darlinghurst Road, there was little joy in that. They were temporary affairs and left a feeling of defeat. If this was all that being a free woman had to offer, what was it that the feminists got so worked up about?

Then I met Mona van Wein. She lived in the Wintergarden in Darlinghurst Road, which still has a number of brass plates announcing the presence of some members of the medical profession—a dentist, a radiologist, and a physiotherapist—on its upper floors. Mona was one of the last. She was a lady of boundless energy, good will and considerable charm, though no longer in her first youth—a fact that worried her a lot. She is the only woman I have ever known who wore a brassiere when she went to bed. She had a large circle of acquaintances and held 'open house' on Tuesday nights, where anyone who cared to come was welcome to drink a glass of wine, nibble a few biscuits, and participate in what were usually discussions of a rather higher intellectual level than usual. Not to have been to one of Mona's Tuesday nights was to have missed something that was intrinsically The Cross. It was through Guido and Ula that I became one of the regulars, and thanks to them that I met a number of unusual and interesting people I might otherwise have missed.

For example, there was Friedel Fink. Friedel and Lotte, his wife, and their two children had fled from Berlin and the horrors of the Third Reich shortly before World War II broke out and, having failed to get a permit to migrate to America, chose Australia in preference to South Africa where aparthied seemed as great a threat as the swastika. Lotte was a gynaecologist who had earned herself an enviable reputation in Berlin, and Friedel enjoyed the distinction of being a psychoanalyst who had gone to Vienna and learnt his skill from Sigmund Freud himself. In spite of which, neither he nor Lotte were considered qualified to practise in Australia, so he had accepted a minor job in the mental hospital at Morisset while Lotte remained in Macleay Street, practiced illegally and helped to educate their children and bring comfort to many of her women friends.

Lotte was a brisk and rather overbearing woman who was openly scornful of a pretty little Viennese lady by the name of Lisel. Whether Friedel had met Lisel during his apprenticeship with Sigmund Freud or not, I do not know, but that he was extremely fond of her and had induced her to follow him out to Australia is beyond all doubt. She remained discreetly in the background and Friedel never referred to her, but whenever Lotte did she always prefixed her remark by calling her 'that stupid Lisel'. Which was unjust, as Lisel was a charming and highly intelligent woman.

Morisset is not a great distance from Sydney, and Friedel always managed to be present on Mona's Tuesday nights, but when he was transferred to the mental hospital at Orange the distance was too great. As Lotte was too engaged in her illegal practice and caring for the two children to visit him very often, she took a vixenish pleasure in persuading certain of her women friends to visit him for the weekend just to annoy 'that stupid Lisel.' When my turn came I said that I would go, not from any wish to annoy poor Lisel, but because I was attracted to the thought of spending a short time in an insane asylum. Jorgensen had told me that a writer should look in every door, and this was a door that I had never expected to be allowed to look through. It was an interesting experience.

The asylum was some distance from the town and consisted of a number of red brick barracks, all of them stark and ugly with iron bars before each window and faces that peered from behind the bars and sometimes grimaced and uttered animal cries as I went past. These cries were at their loudest when the moon was full. Not far inside the entrance gates was a single-storey building that looked a little less forbidding than its neighbours, perhaps because its windows were unbarred. Through them I could see a number of men and women who seemed to be waiting for something to happen. Some of them moved restlessly about the room, others sat staring ahead with no expression on their faces. I asked Friedel who they were and what they were waiting for.

'They're waiting to be admitted,' he said. 'They've not yet been certified and are under observation.' Poor wretches, no wonder they looked already damned.

Friedel occupied a small brick cottage that was reasonably comfortable but lacked all pretentions to being a home. There were no curtains on the windows, no carpets on the floor, no cushions on the chairs. Two identical women arrived each morning to do the household chores. They were of an indefinable age, both wore shapeless dresses, thick black cotton stockings, running shoes with rubber soles and knitted caps pulled down to their eyebrows. If the purpose had been to rob them of all identity, to turn them into creatures devoid of hope, those horrible clothes succeeded admirably. Yet they showed some signs of life. I was a novelty and they were delighted that something had happened to brighten the routine of their lives. Where did I come from, what was my name, and what did I do? they wanted to know. When I told them I came from Sydney and wrote plays for radio, one of them grew animated.

'I write for radio,' she said. 'You can hear me every day. All over the world. I had a letter from the Prince of Wales, thanking me. What do you think of that?'

I said I thought it was remarkable and that I envied her success. I wondered if I would become like her if I went on writing for *Dr Mac*.

Orange is noted for the blistering heat of its summer. I was there in February and before I went to bed would take a shower. On the second night of my visit I came back to my room to find Friedel already in the bed. I was totally unprepared for this, as there had been no suggestion of such a thing either then or at any other time. I liked him, I admired his intellect, enjoyed the discussions we had, but as a man he simply did not exist. Now, there he was, stark naked, lying in my bed expecting me to join him there.

'Don't be nervous, Betty,' he said. Nervous! Me!!!

I was annoyed at finding myself in such a situation and not sure how to deal with it. To adopt an attitude of outraged virtue would make me appear ridiculous. He was fully aware of my past, and my present was no secret either, as I had told him about Nick and the men in B Company and he had said I had made a mistake in sending Nick away. How was I to send *him* away without creating a scene? Perhaps it was best to take the easy way and save a lot of fuss. So I got into bed with him. He would not let me put out the light, which further irritated me and things were not progressing very well when he slipped his hand behind my head and raised it off the pillow. I thought he was going to kiss me instead of which he struck me a stinging blow across the cheek. I was out on the floor in an instant, raving at him, furious.

'What's the matter with you? Why did you do it?' I asked when I had cooled down a bit.

'I thought that you were laughing at me,' was his reply.

Then my anger died. This disciple of Sigmund Freud, this authority on other people's problems, had the smallest penis of any man that I had ever known. Poor Friedel, he must have been extremely sensitive about it and that explained his sudden fit of anger. Perhaps I had been guilty of a faint smile, but it was not intentional, nor had I been taken by surprise. Mona had stayed with him while he was still at Morisset and had told me about his handicap.

I did not cut short my visit and any awkwardness that may have resulted from this embarrassing affair was avoided when an attractive young woman arrived the following day. She was surprised to find that Friedel was not alone but was not in any way put out. She was a psychiatric nurse and had worked with him at Morisset, so they had a lot to talk about. Her name was Cynthia and I learnt that she was the sister of the John Reed I had heard so much about at the time of the Ern Malley hoax. Late in the afternoon she drove away and none of us then guessed that she was Sidney Nolan's future wife.

The next two days passed peacefully. Friedel was his usual imperturbable self and I learnt a little about the subconscious mind, vide Sigmund Freud. For example: I accidentally knocked his elbow when he was lighting a cigarette and scattered the matches on the floor.

'Don't be resentful, Betty,' he said with a smile.

'Resentful! I?'

'That's how Freud would interpret what you just did.'

This seemed a little far-fetched to me. There was more sense in what Friedel had to say about the inadvisability of a writer undergoing deep analysis.

'Never be tempted to do it,' he said. 'I had ambitions to be a writer when I was young and had met with some success but after being analysed by Freud, I dried up altogether. I was always analysing myself and asking what subconscious motives had inspired my plots. Absolutely fatal!'

There were many occasions since then when I have been tempted to unburden myself on an analyst's couch but resisted the urge to do so. Not only because of Friedel's words, but mainly because the price of such self-indulgence is very high. When I was most in need of help, I had not the money to pay for it, when I had the money the need for help had passed, which did not prevent me from reading the works of Adler, Freud, and Margaret Mead, which helped me regain my sanity and did my writing no harm.

It was probably Friedel who introduced Norman Haire to Mona's little world. Whoever it was, Norman added greatly to the interest of those Tuesday nights and enabled me to get to know an extraordinary man and look upon him as a friend. There is no doubt that Ethel Mannin in her book, *Confessions and Impressions,* had not exaggerated when she described the glittering life that he had led in London, the house in Harley Street with its Chinese screens and priceless Persian rugs, the sterling silver dinner-service, and the 'richly coloured dragons writhing on the ceiling of his consulting room'. But he never moaned about the vanished past, its glories and its pleasures as so many other emigrés were wont to do, and he fitted into Mona's rather shabby little flat with commendable ease. He also did not complain about the limitations of the flat he occupied in Ithaca Road, a mere stone's throw from the one I had in The Raymond, and as for the gourmet meals that had done so much to ruin his figure, he cooked a simple dinner on a gas stove and relied on his friends to invite him to a meal more in keeping with his past.

He was a diabetic and would come prepared for the consequences of overindulgence with a syringe and phial of insulin. These he would set out on a spotless white linen cloth, and then gorge himself to repletion on the forbidden fruits. His only sign of ostentation was the manservant that he kept, but Vincent was a necessity, as Norman never trusted himself to drive a car and, as he never had a wife or a woman to attend to his other needs, Vincent no doubt performed these functions as well.

Ethel Mannin revealed the fact that the medical profession was not Norman's chosen field—he had wanted to be an actor and only consideration for his parents had induced him to adopt the less hazardous career. He told me about this himself on one of the occasions when I was bidden to Ithaca Road to share a prawn omelette with him. (No wine. He smoked like a chimney, but alcohol of any kind was strictly taboo.) It appears that he had met a well-known actor, Oscar Asche who, though born in Grenfell, New South Wales, had met with spectacular success in London and was paying a brief visit to Australia. Having seen Norman play Mercutio in a student performance at Sydney High, the great man had been so impressed that he offered to take him back to London and use his influence to further his progress there.

'It broke my heart to refuse,' said Norman, on the verge of tears even after forty years and his triumphs in Harley Street.

Therefore it was no surprise when he announced that he was going to play some roles in Doris Fitton's Independent Theatre in North Sydney. He made his debut in Shaw's *Saint Joan*, in which Doris had cast him as the Bishop of Beauvais. It was typecasting in the extreme, as Norman had both the figure and the presence with which to portray the arrogant prince of the church. In order to do it justice, he had squandered a whole year's clothing coupons on yards and yards of scarlet silk, which he had made up into a robe of suitable proportions. Unfortunately he had managed to antagonise some other members of the cast by his overbearing manner, and they avenged themselves by putting an empty petrol tin on the tail of the splendid garment while he was standing in the wings waiting to make his spectacular first entrance. The banging and clatter that accompanied him totally ruined what should have been an impressive moment and the audience showed its delight with laughter and loud applause. Poor Norman was deeply hurt, and threatened to resign but Doris made the culprits beg his pardon, and honour was appeased.

His next role was that of the butler in *The Admirable Crichton*. After that, I think his enthusiasm dwindled, as I do not remember him appearing in anything else. But he did appear quite regularly at Mona's and was treated with due respect.

In spite of all his bombast, I think he was a lonely man, else why did he invite me to share a prawn omelette with him? And when Guido and Ula went to live at Newport Beach, he seemed glad to spend the weekend in their modest little house. This, despite the swarms of mosquitoes and bush flies, the long climb uphill from the beach, and the lack of indoor sanitation. This last he found to be particularly trying. It was a rare sight to see his fat pink body emerging from the surf wearing the briefest V's and a rubber bathing cap to keep the water out of his ears. Wrapping a towel about his loins, he would stride away in this semi-naked state, oblivious to startled looks. Bikinis had not yet been dreamed up in 1946.

There was what might be termed a shifting population at Mona's, and few of the faces seen there remain in my memory today. Norman Haire and the Finks are exceptions, so is a stocky little man from Budapest called Andrew Ungar. Andrew was an analytical chemist who had arrived in Australia with not much more than his degree in science but who now had a thriving laboratory in which, among other things, he manufactured male and female hormones. The best male hormones, so he told me, were distilled from the urine of young men, particularly soldiers, so he received a regular supply from the Victoria barracks in Paddington. I never learnt the source of his raw material for the female variety.

In contrast to Andrew's optimism there was Tommy Challon's gloom. Tommy was a cartoonist for the *Daily Telegraph* and lived not far from me in Elizabeth Bay. I used to see him every morning plodding up the hill on his way to the *Telegraph*, with his folio under his arm containing sketches of some rough ideas for the next day's issue. They had to be witty as well as relevant to current political events. The obligation to be witty every day was what made Tommy so depressed. He had my sympathy, having vivid recollections of the time when I had been asked to write a half-hour comedy for 2GB which would be broadcast the following week. In desperation I had bought a book called *Jokes for All Occasions* and when I mentioned this to Tommy he had said: 'For god's sake lend it to me.' Later, when he brought it back he told me very sadly that, though he had read every page, he had not been able to raise a smile. Poor Tommy, he had once dreamed of being a great musician as I had dreamed of being a great playwright; he had once played first violin in a leading orchestra as I had had my moment when *The Touch of Silk* was performed in 1928. Now both of us had failed to grasp our star and both of us were depressed.

I do not remember when Hans Erickson first appeared at one of Mona's Tuesday gatherings, but well recall the sensation he caused, especially among the women there, including myself. He came in one night, tall, blond and so outstandingly good-looking that, to me, he reduced all the other males in the room to insignificance. It was by no means love at first sight—love and Hans Ericksson were mutually exclusive. It was my appreciation of physical perfection that held me spellbound, though I made no effort to attract his attention, being content to sit and look at him from time to time and wonder who and what he was.

His Norwegian origin was obvious; he had the blue eyes and magnificent physique of his race, and a faint rolling of his r's that lent a pleasant variation to his speech. Even the men in the room seemed impressed by him.

Norman Haire was visibly excited, especially when he learned that he and Hans were neighbours. By some means known only to himself, Hans had managed to acquire a flat in a house that was tucked away on the edge of the little park at the bottom of Ithaca Road which provided the maximum of privacy that his enigmatic nature seemed to demand. It also gave easy access to the little pier and the boats that were moored, which was an important consideration since he made a living buying and selling boats. How far the acquaintance with Norman Haire progressed I do not know, but I was content to watch Hans sitting indolently in his chair and admire him from a distance. To me, he spelt danger as a tiger lurking in a thicket might warn one to keep away. It is easy to picture my surprise when, one night, round about midnight, he appeared at my door. I had answered his knock without the least idea of who the late visitor might be and, in my surprise, said the obvious thing.

'Hans! Is anything wrong? What do you want?'

'What do you think I want?' was the also obvious reply.

I had the same feeling of bewilderment and disbelief that had paralysed my ability to think clearly when Alan Marshall's crutches had come padding towards my room, and when I had found Friedel Fink in my bed—though Friedel would say that I had subconsciously willed it so and that this explains my readiness to acquiesce. I am inclined to agree, but few women would have turned Hans Erickson away when he came knocking at their door. Not this woman, anyhow.

Without his clothes he was even more spectacular than he was when fully dressed, and when the last garment fell to the floor I felt that I had the Apollo Belvedere and Michelangelo's David standing in front of me.

In my varied experience of men I have met some who were nervous and had difficulty in achieving their objective but, with a little help and encouragement had managed to succeed; some who had the misfortune to be the victims of premature ejaculation, which caused much embarrassment to us both, two who were completely impotent and could not be helped, and Hans, who was singular in that he seemed unable to reach the desired conclusion of the act.

It was an experience not to be forgotten, nor to be recommended. Again and again, I thought the moment of release had come, in the end I prayed it would. I was exhausted, even a little afraid, as he was driven to the point of frenzy and grew violent. Once or twice, I thought that he would strangle me, but finally the paroxysm came. It took him a while to recover. Then he got up and dressed himself, gave me a brief kiss, and went.

Imperturbable as ever, he was at Mona's again next week and by an unspoken agreement, neither of us gave any indication that we were more than mere acquaintances. But I got a lot of satisfaction from knowing that only I, of all the other women in the room, knew what lay under those casual clothes and enigmatic expression. Or did I? How would I know on whose door he knocked at midnight? Nor did I care. He came and went, not often and with intervals long enough for me to recover and grow curious about what the cause of his problem might be. But neither Sigmund Freud nor Margaret Mead were any help to me. Needless to say, I did not seek the answer from Friedel.

Then he disappeared. Nobody knew what had become of him until there was the report in the paper of a yacht that had run aground on the coast near Bateman's Bay. There were three people on board, one of whom was Hans. He had managed to swim ashore but the other two had drowned. There was an enquiry, of course, and Hans gave evidence that he had been hired to sail the boat to Tasmania by the couple who had been drowned. He had sold the boat to them a short time previously and, as they were inexperienced, had agreed to see them safely through the hazardous voyage. No blame was attached to him for the disaster as he had been asleep below decks when the boat ran on the reef and there was no reason to doubt his word. He had told me that he made a living by buying and selling boats and then, as often as not, being paid a handsome sum to teach the novice yachtsmen how to manage their newest toy. But was that the sole source of his income? His proximity to the jetty at the foot of Ithaca Road and the current laxness of customs officials were an invitation to engage in more profitable pursuits. Who knows?

A curious incident occurred some two years after this. Guido and Ula were living at Newport Beach and I often went and stayed with them. One hot night I went for a swim, not unaccompanied I confess, and did not get back till late. The water had been milk warm and the phosphorus had clung to our limbs and mingled with our hair and the waves were studded with stars as they washed along the shore. It was an enchanted night and we were in no hurry to cut it short.

When I got back to the house I looked for my watch which I had taken off and laid on a table immediately inside an open window. It was no longer there. Ula has put it away for safety, I thought, and went to bed. But Ula had never seen it, nor could it be found. 'I can't be sure,' said Guido thoughtfully, 'but I'll swear I saw Hans Erickson last night. He was waiting for a bus.'

I never found my watch, but it was insured and I used the money to pave the courtyard at the house in Castlecrag.

Apart from the valiant Lotte Fink, few of the women at Mona's left any lasting impression on me, but there was one, a somewhat vague but excessively friendly woman of middle age who attracted my attention, not on the score of her intellect but because she was an astrologer. Her interest quickened as soon as she heard that I had been born on the twenty-second of July and even without my asking her, volunteered to cast my horoscope. The result of her deliberations came as a surprise. I have long since lost the complicated chart she handed me, as I did not take it very seriously, but certain parts of it stay in my memory, mainly because the prognostications proved to be so accurate.

Here, in effect, is what it said: Being born in mid-afternoon of the twenty-second of July, I was under the influence of two of the most powerful signs in the Zodiac, Cancer and Leo, therefore was assured of an unusual life. But Jupiter, benign, beneficent Jupiter, was in the ascendant as well; consequently, no matter what disaster I suffered, I would always manage to survive. But I had Saturn to contend with—he brings disappointments and delays, he moves slowly through the firmament and he would be there most of my life. But Jupiter would triumph in the end, and in my final years I would have success and happiness. I was adverse to the sign of Libra and would have difficulty in forming lasting relationships with other people, and finally my Venus was in Virgo, so I would have long periods of chastity in my life.

This last prediction caused me some amusement, as chastity, prolonged or otherwise, seemed very remote at the time.

I find it difficult to reconcile the woman that I am now with the woman of those tumultuous years. I ask myself what it was that drove me to such excesses, what it was that I was searching for, and what did I achieve?

There is no simple answer. Primarily I think that I was searching for a permanent relationship that would replace the one that I had been deprived of, though Kings Cross was not a good place in which to look for it. There was also the strong biological urge, which was fully gratified but brought me no peace or happiness, rather the reverse. All it did was help restore my damaged self-esteem by knowing that I had not lost my power to attract the men. But what kind of men? None of them in any way measured up to the standard Guido had set for me, and with him constantly in front of me, the image could not fade. I should not have come to the Cross, yet being as I am, where else was I to go?

There was another element in the reckless way I went from man to man: a deep inner resentment at having been forced out of the comfortable cocoon of domesticity and into the role of being the sole support of my child. I was now the breadwinner and had to traffic in the marketplace and return with the spoils. In other words, the pay envelope. Having been forced to accept the disadvantages of being a man, was I not then entitled to the advantages? So, when the urge was on me, I was free to gratify it, coldly and dispassionately as a man would do when going to a brothel. In which case, Kings Cross was the place for me to be.

It was confused thinking, self-defeating and extremely hazardous. Even Norman Haire was a little perturbed when I gave him an account of some of my adventures. He warned me of the dangers of VD, of which I was fully aware and which on a number of occasions prompted me to make the biological urge give way to caution. For example, there was the Norwegian sailor Olaf Pedersen.

He was standing on the corner of Market Street waiting for a tram—there were still trams in Sydney then—and was obviously very drunk. He leaned against a light pole and had a wilted carnation in his hand. I had been at a Christmas party; George Edwards and Nell Stirling made it a standard practice. Everyone had been there, everyone who was in any way associated with their production team, and everyone with the exception of myself had appeared to be having a marvellous time. I had gone alone, which always made me feel depressed.

As a mark of their esteem I had been given a place at the top table, presided over by Nell and George, who distributed smiles and goodwill to everyone. Two by two, the couples got up to dance until there was only George and myself and a row of empty chairs. He looked decidedly uneasy, glanced at me and seemed to be on the point of asking me to dance, but I ended his dilemma by getting up and going to the powder room. I didn't shed any tears of self-pity, though I felt like doing so. Instead, I made my way through the crowd and left. And there on the corner of the street was Olaf Pedersen, all six feet of him, propped against the pole, the wilted carnation in his hand.

'Six thousand miles avay from Norvay, and I vish that I vos dere,' he proclaimed in a loud voice.

Something touched my heart. He was so lonely, so unhappy, and so was I.

'What's the matter, sailor?' I asked. He was about to reply when a taxi came along. By a miracle, it was empty. 'Would you like to come with me?'

His face lit up with astonishment but he lost no time in joining me and we were on our way to the Cross.

It happened a long time ago and the details are now blurred, but I can remember helping him up the stairs and making him drink black coffee. Of course, he was intent on going to bed with me, but I had no similar wish. He found it difficult to understand my motive in refusing him but gradually he sobered up a little and grew less aggressive. He asked about myself and prowled about the room, picking up a book and pausing at Gilda's picture hanging on the wall, and said 'That's your bulwark'. I agreed.

He was a member of the crew of an oil tanker, just about

the least desirable and most dangerous occupation any seaman can engage in when a war such as the present one was raging. He was due to sail the following day and I watched him stumble down the stairs and felt sorry I had let him go uncomforted. Months afterwards, I had a letter from him. He was then on the Atlantic run and wrote rather wistfully about the time we met in Sydney and wished 'dat he vas dere.' I never heard from him again and the chance that a torpedo from a German submarine had silenced him is good.

Norman Haire commended me for my discretion. 'Norwegian sailors are notorious for having syphilis,' he said.

Then there was the American Sergeant of Marines. Troop ships and naval vessels were frequently anchored off Rushcutters Bay and the men would be ferried ashore on cutters that ran a shuttle service to the jetty at the foot of Ithaca Road, which meant that they had to pass the door of The Raymond on their way up to the Cross and again as they returned. One night, as I was walking down Elizabeth Bay Road, I became aware of heavy footsteps coming after me. Those were civilised days, despite the war, and the sound of pursuing footsteps did not chill a woman's blood, nor did the voice that said, 'Hi miss, what's the hurry? Got to catch a train or sumpin?'

All I did was walk a little faster. 'Gee, you must be training for a race,' continued the impudent voice. By now he was walking level with me. He was a hulking figure with a roguish look on his quite attractive face, a cap on the side of his head and massive combat boots ringing on the pavement.

We were now at the point where the road swings to the right and continues its downward course towards Ithaca Road. The Raymond was only a few feet away. There was nothing to prevent me from answering that roguish smile and taking him inside, but something in me said: 'Don't!' It was as though a warning bell had rung, so I crossed the road until I reached the door. 'What's the matter? You got a husband or sumthin' in there?' he asked. 'Something,' I replied. 'And I'll bet it's pretty good at that,' were his final words as I put the key in the lock. He would probably have passed any Wasserman test with honours, but that I will never know.

It was a different story with Heinrich von Hamburgh. That wasn't his name, but he insisted that it was. It was VE Day, the war in Europe was finally at an end and I was sitting rather dejectedly in a tram after spending the evening among the frenzied crowd that was celebrating victory. I was dejected because, once again, I had been made aware of my solitary state—it is difficult to celebrate anything by oneself. The paper hats, the flags, the coloured streamers had made me feel depressed, so I failed to notice the man at the far end of the tram who stared at me and followed me as I got out. He said: 'Goodnight', and I looked at him for the first time.

He was dressed in a dark blue sweater and dark pants; the sweater had a crew neck which made me think he was a seaman of some sort, but I was mistaken. He had been released that day from the concentration camp in which he had spent the past four years as an enemy alien.

'Four years without a woman,' so he told me as we sat on the top of a low stone wall on the corner of Macleay Street. He had noticed me in the tram and thought 'wonderful woman type' and decided he would try his luck with me.

The thought of being the woman who would experience the pent-up force of a man who had been deprived for so long excited me, but I was wary and evaded him. He pleaded with me to change my mind. How he pleaded, and with what eloquence! There was something of the poet in him, which further helped his cause, so my resistance grew steadily less and eventually gave way. The warning signal may have sounded, but I did not listen to it. Not that I got venereal disease in any of its forms, but I did get a man who refused to be dismissed when I had had enough of him.

He would wait for me as I came home, would be lurking at the corner of the street as I went out, would come knocking at the door when I wanted to work, and I grew afraid to look out the window in case I saw him staring at me from the fire-escape. I went to the police, but got little sympathy.

'What's he done? Assaulted you? Do you want to lay a charge?'

'No. He follows me about.'

The answer was a shrug and a withering glance.

Once we were walking in Victoria Street and he pointed to the basement of one of the dilapidated buildings there. Evidently that was where he had a room. He tried every way he knew to persuade me to go down the steps with him, but a sudden panic made me refuse to do so. I don't know why I felt that sense of menace; he had never been violent, just persistent, a nuisance more than anything else. But something evil seemed to emanate from that darkened room. I could picture nameless horrors, and tried to break away, but he held me firmly by the arm. Then a taxi came along and I hailed it. The grip on my arm slackened enough for me to break away and open the taxi door. He leaped in after me and I had the wit to tell the driver to take me to the nearest police station. That had the desired effect. Heinrich von Hamburgh leapt out as smartly as he had leapt in and the last I saw of him was standing on the kerb staring after the taxi as it drove away.

I never saw him again. I sometimes wondered why the threat of the police was enough to scare him away. It might have had something to do with his recent release from the concentration camp, that he was under surveillance and might be sent back to Germany if he proved troublesome. What if he had got drunk that night and been arrested with the same result. What did it matter to me? I was free of him and had been taught a sharp lesson.

It was not a pretty incident and I only record it because it illustrates the kind of folly a 'fully liberated' woman can be guilty of. Not every woman, however liberated, would behave with the reckless disregard of consequences that I displayed during those frenzied war years, nor would I advise her to—she might lack 'kind beneficent Jupiter' to watch over her! How I managed to

93

emerge unscathed I do not know, but I did, and I can't help feeling that I became a better person because of the things I learned about my fellow creatures in the process. Be that as it may, it explains why Kings Cross does not surprise or repel me; it is an integral part of myself.

I did not tell Norman Haire about Heinrich von Hamburgh. He was busily engaged in packing up prior to his return to Harley Street.

CHAPTER 11

The war in Europe might have been at an end but the one in the Pacific was definitely not, though its character had undergone a change. The Japanese were now in full retreat, General MacArthur had fulfilled his promise to the Philippines to return and drive them out, and his immaculately tailored men had been replaced in Sydney by the men of His Majesty's Royal Navy. And a sorry sight they were. Instead of the rounded buttocks and well-nourished cheeks of the GI's there were the pasty faces and hollow chests of Birmingham and the East End. Their jackets were not tailored but mass produced and did not fit, square-cut at the neck so that scrawny throats and hollow collarbones were pitilessly revealed.

Equally pitiless was the effect on them of the strong Australian beer. Taken unawares and with thirsts accumulated during long weeks at sea, they succumbed at the third glass. The sight of them lying in the doorways, lurching along the street and vomiting in the gutters, was a sorry spectacle. Coupled with this was their miserly pay, so there was a mass exodus of *filles de joie* to Brisbane, where the affluent GI's still lingered and offered rewards no longer possible in Sydney.

There was a marked cooling off in the Cross, which extended itself to me. I had learnt the futility of casual encounters. What had I gained from them? Nothing but a temporary appeasing of the hunger that had tormented me. It was still there, but to a lesser degree. But the wish for permanence was in no way diminished. I no longer enjoyed my right to behave like a man and take my pleasure where I found it; in other words, I was heartily sick of my much vaunted freedom and was only too ready to exchange it for the bondage of the wedding ring. I would look at stolid, ageing couples walking hand in hand along the street, or sitting comfortably side by side in the park, and envy them. They had weathered the storms and tempests of their youth, had not quit as I had done when something not to my liking had occurred and this comforting companionship was their reward. Who did I have to comfort me? No-one. I was, once again, succumbing to self-pity.

The activities of the past two years were made possible by the fact that, during the week, Gilda was safely billeted with Mrs Chapman. Weekends she spent with me, during which I reverted to my normal self. No man was permitted to intrude on our two days together. On Sunday afternoon I would take her back to Wahroonga and drink afternoon tea with Mrs Chapman, before returning to the Cross and another five days at the typewriter.

This routine came to an end when Neura sold 'Larnoo' and had the grace to give Guido a share of the price. Ula was then quite ill. Her work at the munitions factory and the wretched little flat in Darlinghurst Road had had an adverse effect on her and she had developed a nervous rash that made her life a misery, so Guido had bought the house at Newport Beach that I have already spoken of. Ula's daughter, Deirdre, was an additional reason for this. She, poor child, had been sent to boarding school when the time at Kirby's farm had come to an end, and was desperately unhappy there. Now she could live with her mother again and be her usual light-hearted self. There was room in the house for Gilda as well and, while she had not been unhappy with Mrs Chapman, she was thrilled to be with her father again and have Deidre to go to school with instead of the rather patronising Louana.

It was not without reluctance that I agreed to this new arrangement. Gilda, like most small girls, was starting to show a preference for her father, which I thought was most unfair. He had done so little for her, I so much. But how was she to know? I could have refused to let her go and left her with Mrs Chapman, but that would have denied her the sense of belonging to a family that Newport could provide and I could not. Guido had said that if losing both of us was the price he had to pay for Ula—'price beyond measure' were his words—he was prepared to pay it. If I let Gilda go and live at Newport he would have her and Ula too, without paying any price at all.

I must have talked to Friedel Fink about my problem as I can remember him telling me that to deprive her of her father could have serious future results.

'On no account ever try to poison her mind against him, no matter how badly he has behaved,' he warned. 'That is the surest way of turning her into a lesbian.'

A statement open to question, of course, but it had its effect on me. I put up no further opposition and caught the bus to Newport on Friday afternoons instead of the train to Wahroonga, for which I received my reward. I had the comforting feeling of belonging to a family; Gilda blossomed like a flower and has certainly shown no marked preference for members of the female sex.

It was during this cosy period that Leading Aircraftsman James McClelland came back on leave from Melville Island. We had corresponded more or less regularly during the time he had been away and I was unreservedly glad to see him. His time in Sydney was brief, as he had spent the greater part of his leave in Melbourne, visiting his family and, I gathered, renewing past friendships and an old romance, though who the lady was I did not know. Nor did I enquire, but it was undoubtedly she who accounted for a certain coolness on Jim's part, which I had not anticipated. He also showed a preference for conducting a polemic with Guido on the theories of Karl Marx when he should have been paying attention to me.

At the time I was friendly with a girl called Claire who was living in the so-called castle on Bungen Head, overlooking Newport Beach. It was an untidy heap of stone and had been unoccupied for years and how Claire came to be there all by herself was a mystery. She had a husband somewhere in New Guinea and took his absence very lightly, as she had an American captain staying with her on this occasion, no doubt to scare away the ghosts that undoubtedly haunted the place.

I told her about the resistance I had met with from Jim, and she suggested that both of us should come and have a few preliminary drinks before taking him down to the beach and letting nature take its course.

'He'll make love to me tonight if I have to rape him,' I said.

The place was dimly lit by a kerosene lamp, the wind howled round the crumbling walls and the four of us sat consuming gin, or bourbon, while the American captain sat at Claire's feet and stroked her leg and grew more and more amorous with every drink. It soon became clear that we were no longer welcome, so Jim and I got up to go and by the time we reached the beach it was clear that his resistance to me had been considerably reduced. It was one of those nights that linger in the memory and I was surprised when he made no mention of it in his book, *Stirring the Possum*.

My feelings for him had undergone a change—perhaps that night on the beach had lit the fire that had been missing before— and he was no longer just one of the men who had made love to me, but a man I began to dream about and yearn for much in the same way I had yearned for Nick. It had also appeared to have made an impression on him, as he wrote more frequently and ardently, and I lost all wish to resume the promiscuous way of life that I had found so futile. Therefore I was totally unprepared for a remark he made in one of his letters to me.

'I think I am in love with you and if you were ten years younger I would ask you to marry me.'

Of course, he was right. I was then forty-one years old and he was twenty-nine, but it was a horrible awakening. Though totally unaware of it he had told me I was finished, and consigned me to the scrap heap. Good enough to go to bed with but not to marry. I took it very hard, but concealed my feelings and continued to write as I had done before, so he had not the least idea of what he had done when the war came to an end and he came back in August 1945.

I was back in the house at Castlecrag and stood at the open door and watched him coming down the hill, a ragged, emaciated figure that had none of the swagger of former days. He and a handful of other Australians had been left behind on Manus Island when the Americans went home at the conclusion of hostilities. Because of their knowledge of radar, which the Americans then lacked, they had been seconded to them for the duration. Now that there was no further need of them, they had been abandoned and apparently forgotten. Nobody remembered them for several months and they had almost starved to death before they were collected and brought back to Sydney. He phoned me on arrival and told me he was coming out to Castlecrag.

There is no mention of that in his book, instead it merely states that when he got back to Sydney he had only two friends: Laurie Short and Laurie's wife, Nancy Borlase.

When did I cease to be a friend? Perhaps it was after we had a row a week or so after he had come wearily down the hill. It was in late January, which can be a trying month in Sydney with thunderstorms and sudden bursts of sunshine creating a hothouse that strains the nerves to breaking point. I react badly to excessive heat, and that summer was one of the worst. I also had to keep on working despite the discomfort of prickly heat and a feeling of exhaustion. During the day Jim would go off on his own affairs, but he would come back at night. At first I was glad to have him, but as well as the prickly heat that letter also rankled, and the welcome grew less and less as the days went on.

He was due to leave at the end of the second week and I looked forward to the time when he would go, so when he came in one night and casually announced that he had changed his mind and proposed to stay for a few more days, my self-control gave way. What words passed between us I can't recall, but they were short and to the point, and Diamond Jim went back up the hill, no doubt to seek consolation with Laurie Short.

It was quite some time before I saw him again. He was studying law at Sydney University and was dancing with a fellow-student whom he subsequently married. Our eyes met and we exchanged a smile and went on dancing as before.

CHAPTER 12

If the lady who cast horoscopes had been reading my chart just then, she would have seen that Saturn was about to suffer an eclipse and that Jupiter was in the ascendant. In sober terms, Alan Williamson was about to re-enter my life after an absence of fifteen years.

Alan was a cheerful little Englishman who arrived in Melbourne in 1932 to further the interests of Gaumont British Films, and created some excitement by announcing that, if a suitable story could be found, that august body would consider making a film in Australia and possibly establishing a base here. It was just at the time that Efftee Films were about to cease production and I had written the scenario of a story I had intended to submit to them. Instead, along with many other writers, I sent it to Alan Williamson. Then came the usual weeks of silence and, finally, a letter telling me that my story had been selected to be sent to Gaumont British for approval, and would I please make an appointment to come in and discuss details.

We got on famously right from the start. I was dizzy with excitement and Alan was pleased to be the cause of so much happiness. Nevertheless, he warned me not to be too optimistic.

'These things take time, you know. You'll need a lot of patience.'

Prophetic words! Week after week went by and still no word from Gaumont British. I ceased to telephone and ask for news and busied myself with other things. Guido Baracchi was one of them; my decision to leave my husband and elope with him was another. Just before I did so, I went to tell Alan what I intended to do.

'When you get to London, telephone my brother,' he said. 'He supplies most of the raw film to the British film industry and will know what the position is with Gaumont British.' After he had wished me good luck and planted a friendly kiss on my cheek, we said goodbye.

But there was no good news for me in London, only a regretful voice telling me that no decision had been reached, but not to give up hope. I hung up the receiver with a feeling of finality. It was to be Guido and Moscow and not London and Gaumont British Films. Now, after fifteen years, Alan Williamson was once again in Australia, this time representing Ealing Studios, which had sent Harry Watt ahead of him to begin the preliminaries to making a film called *The Overlanders*. I am not quite sure when or how I met Alan Williamson again, but I can clearly recall his first words:

'Betty! Where on earth have you been? We searched London for you in 1933. There was a contract with Gaumont British ready for you to sign, but you had disappeared.'

I had indeed disappeared, into Soviet Russia, leaving no forwarding address. So *The Flying Doctor* was made instead of my story *Greater Love*, and my one great chance of 'breaking into films' was at an end. Game and rubber to Saturn!

But Jupiter had brought me Alan Williamson. I had been aware of his interest fifteen years ago in Melbourne, but then there had been no place in my life for anyone but Guido. Now there was an aching, empty void, and Alan Williamson was the man who filled it. There was none of the fervour there had been with Guido but a quiet feeling of fulfilment, even peace, as though I had reached shelter after being battered by the storm. It was love, but of a different kind and I was happy in a way that I had never been before.

There was no thought of marriage, as Alan already had a wife and I had no wish to disrupt his life; furthermore, I liked things as they were. They seemed to be quite perfect, the realisation of the liberated woman's dream: a healthy child, a lover I liked, a house of my own and, not by any means the least, financial independence. This last had come about by means of a piece of great good fortune that had recently come my way: I had been asked by the *Sydney Morning Herald* if I would be interested in writing the story, and what dialogue was required, for a daily cartoon-strip on the lines of *Speed Gordon* and *Superman*. I said I was extremely interested and was soon in receipt of a weekly cheque that continually astonished me. Compared to the amount of time required to deliver five radio scripts a week, *The Conways*, which ran for several years, seemed like child's play and left me with ample time to enjoy the house at Castlecrag and my new relationship with Alan Williamson.

I knew he had a wife who lived in the Blue Mountains and, though he seldom mentioned her, I gathered that she was an invalid and seldom left the house, so while he spent the weekends with her, the weekdays, when all the interesting things took place, were his own, and if Alan met a need in my life, I did the same in his. Contrary to other married men that I had known, he made no effort to conceal his involvement with me. He took me to the theatre, to dinner at Ushers or the Australia Hotel, as well as to previews of films such as *Kind Hearts and Coronets, The Third Man, Colonel Blimp* and other classics of the golden age of British films. It was the kind of life that I had been deprived of recently and had sorely missed.

Alan had had a long acquaintance with film making, his father having been one of the pioneers of the English industry, and had come out to Australia in 1911 at the request of Cousins and Spencer—two of the earliest names in Australian films— in order to produce and direct both *Captain Moonlight* and its sequel *Captain Midnight*, neither of which survived the test of public exhibition. Now, in 1947, he was back again. At last there was a thunderous success and, encouraged by this, Michael Balcon, the head of Ealing, told him to proceed with his new pet project, *The Eureka Stockade*. Alan had been sent out to keep an eye on Harry, who was apt to be temperamental and even reckless if left to his own devices.

There was another, even more delicate matter for Alan to negotiate; Ealing Studios, or rather Michael Balcon, was willing to spend a great deal of money in consolidating the now promising

Australian industry, and needed support from Norman Rydge, a powerful figure in the Australian financial world. Rydge was also chairman of Greater Union Theatres, which controlled almost all the channels of film distribution in all states. The deal that Alan was endeavouring to negotiate was mainly concerned with converting the obsolete National Film Studio at Pagewood into a vast complex of studios, sound stages, laboratories, cutting and projection rooms required for a major industry, with Ealing Studios providing 50 per cent of the cost and Norman Rydge the remainder in return for sole distributing rights, both in Australia and overseas, for Greater Union. Rydge was being cagey and the success or otherwise of *Eureka* could well be a deciding factor in the ultimate decision.

I was fully conversant with the problems created by Harry Watt and *The Eureka Stockade*, but had no inkling whatever of the delicate negotiations under way so when Alan rang me up one day and mentioned casually that there had been a hitch about the development at Pagewood, I paid no particular attention to what he said, thinking it referred to Harry Watt and his film. Later in the day when Rex Reinits, co-author of the script, rang up, I said to him quite casually that I had heard there was some problem about the use of Pagewood Studios, where the interior scenes of *Eureka* would be shot.

Rex was instantly alert. He rang Harry Watt and asked what the trouble was; Harry knew nothing about it, so Rex rang someone else, and so the rumour spread, eventually reaching Alan's ears.

He rang as usual next morning and I answered, expecting to hear the usual jovial voice, instead there was one I scarcely recognised.

'Betty, did you tell anyone what I said about Pagewood studios?'

My mouth went dry. 'Yes, I told Rex Reinits.'

'My God!'

'What's the matter? What have I done?'

'It's all right. It can't be helped.'

'But tell me!'

'I can't talk. I'll ring you later on.'

The phone went dead and our happy relationship died as well. The sight of his stricken face when I saw him in a few days' time dried all the words in my throat. There are no words to convey the depth of my remorse at having unwittingly brought disaster on the man for whom I cared so much. He did not reproach me in any way, but his eyes had a hounded look and avoided mine. He would not discuss the matter or give me any indication of the damage I had done, and there seemed to be nothing I could say. Confused and unhappy, I went back to Castlecrag and he went off to try and straighten out the mess that he had been landed in. Soon after that, he was called back to London, which was a relief to both of us. When he came back he made no effort to see me, nor did I try to make contact with him.

In time my feeling of remorse grew less and I began to think that I was not solely to blame for what had occurred. How could a man of Alan's experience tell a woman such a vital piece of information and not warn her to keep silent about it? Nevertheless, I could not dismiss the thought that I might have had something to do with the deal with Norman Rydge falling through and read at a later date that 'as no Australian support for films to be produced at Pagewood was forthcoming, it has been reluctantly decided to close the studio down'.

While I had met with this fresh disaster, my friend Roberta had profited greatly from the unfortunate affair with Alan Williamson. Through his intervention her two boys, Michael and Nicholas, had played leading roles in a children's film, *Bush Christmas*. It was a simple story, shot on a modest budget, and it achieved international acclaim. No-one was more surprised by this than its author and director, Ralph Smart, who had been a co-director in *The Overlanders*. Nicky, then an engaging six-year-old with a gap between his front teeth, literally stole the show in the role of Snow, and became an overnight star.

Roberta had grown bored with ironing Edgar's shirts, polishing the furniture and growing geraniums in a window box and had gone in search of other forms of entertainment. What they were

I never really knew, but there was talk of her going off to town and not coming back at night, leaving Edgar to put the children into bed and wonder where she was. He did not go in search of her, but once he had to hurry into town and bail her out when she got into trouble with the police.

Roberta's trouble lay in her low tolerance of alcohol. The average drinker can consume a considerable amount with no visible effects, but after the second sherry poor Roberta was no longer quite herself. This gave rise to some embarrassing incidents when she gave a party. Basically uncertain of herself, her anxiety would increase as the time for the guests to arrive approached. Had she prepared enough food? Would the chimney smoke? Would Nick refuse to go to sleep and bellow for attention? Had she put salt in the ragout? To boost her confidence she would have a little nip of scotch or a shot of gin, then, perhaps, another, so that by the time the guests arrived, she would be in poor shape to receive them. Once she had to be carried off to bed to sleep it off. Roberta's parties became noted for their unpredictability.

But, thanks to Nicky and his director Ralph Smart, she now had a new source of diversion. As both the children were minors, she could insist that she accompany them when they went on location. She would have given a great deal to be included in the cast, but Ralph had baulked at that, and when *Bush Christmas* was followed by *Bitter Springs* and the more ambitious *Eureka Stockade*, Edgar at least knew where she was, which failed to make him less unhappy than he had been before.

Unlike *Bush Christmas, Bitter Springs* met with only moderate success and Ralph Smart faded from the scene. Nicky, however, became a star of children's radio, and to a less extent of the stage. He played Puck in *A Midsummer Night's Dream*, TylTyl in *The Bluebird*, the lame boy in *The Pied Piper* and had parts in countless serials on the ABC. Edgar had also established a sound reputation for himself as an actor and coached Nicky in his parts, and it was a common sight to see father and son waiting at the bus stop in the evening on their way to radio station 3LO or the Theatre Royal. Roberta found diversion in a number of unspecified ways.

The Conways continued to run its daily course in the *SMH*, bringing in its weekly cheque, and I began to feel the urge to write something more worthwhile in my spare time. *The Touch of Silk* was the only claim that I could make to being a writer of distinction and that had troubled me for a long time. It had been a success, artistic though not financial, and brought me a brief hour of glory which had faded very rapidly. Had it not been for the ABC, which revived it from time to time, both the play and its author would have been forgotten. Now was my time to prove that I was not a 'once only' playwright and that I was worthy of respect.

Unhappily, I met with no success as, even under the ideal conditions that I now enjoyed, the Muse refused to visit me. I agonised and sweated, but to no avail. I lacked a central theme, there was no clear motivation in the situations and the characters I conjured up in my imagination. *The Touch of Silk* had seemed to be inspired by a force outside myself; it had almost written itself and there had been times when it was difficult to keep pace with the ideas that poured into my mind. It had been an exhilarating time and when I went for walks in the evening I had felt that my feet barely touched the ground. Now I limped painfully along the road and seemed to be getting nowhere.

But the Muse had not entirely deserted me. A swarthy gentleman from Peru by the name of Sidney John Kay had been bustling round Sydney in an attempt to establish a theatre, to be sponsored by the brothers J. and N. Tate, where gifted young actors and actresses could display their art in something more rewarding than radio or an occasional season of English drawing-room comedy. Inspired by John, I dramatised some passages out of *Don Quixote*, which he greeted with great enthusiasm and set about casting right away.

John was nothing if not an optimist. He had not yet found a suitable building in which to establish his theatre, but Peter Finch and Leo McKern, both of them still unknown outside

Australia, were cast in the leading roles. John began making a papier mâché model of Rosinante, but despite his frantic efforts to find a suitable venue, none was available, and the lean and hungry Knight of Spain had to remain within the pages of a book. It was a big disappointment to me and, many years later, when I sat in the stalls of a London theatre and watched Keith Michell in *Man of La Mancha*, I thought how much better Peter Finch would have been and that my version of the immortal Don was better than the one I was looking at.

Hope revived, however, when Doris Fitton, of the Independent Theatre, asked if I would revise a dramatised version of *Madame Bovary*. Doris was a truly remarkable woman. She now had a permanent theatre in Miller Street, North Sydney, after years of struggling for survival in different parts of the city despite the handicaps of very little money and the minimum of experience. But what Doris lacked in these respects she made up for in determination and an unshakeable belief in herself. To see her standing in the foyer of the Independent on an opening night, dressed in a low-cut flowing gown, smiling regally to right and left—but only to distinguished patrons—was to see a super-ego in full flower.

I had never received the faintest nod of recognition from her, and was rather in awe of her. Now here was this doyenne of the theatre begging me for help because she had included *Madame Bovary* in the current season's programme without having read it first. She had now discovered that it had a cast of twenty-three and eleven changes of scene.

'Do something about it, *please!*' she implored. 'We start rehearsals at the end of the month and there's nothing to put in its place.'

It was a season of international plays. She had already done Ibsen, Pirandello, Chekhov, Euripides, and Goethe. *Madame Bovary*, with herself in the leading role, was to end a triumphant season. It had been adapted from the original novel by someone who was proficient in French but had a lot to learn about the structure of a play. It was a mishmash of unconnected scenes

108

and unconvincing dialogue, and I could see no way of redeeming it short of a total revision and drastic reduction of scenes, even then it would be a travesty of Flaubert's masterpiece. So I tossed it aside, went into town and searched every bookshop for a copy of the book. By a miracle I found it, then put four sheets of paper in the typewriter, and got to work.

Of course, it was utterly insane. When I had played Helga in *Are You Ready, Comrade?* and raced into the New Theatre League after preparing Guido's dinner, feeding Gilda and putting her to bed, I had thought that even Eleanora Duse could not have been at her best under such conditions. Now I wondered if anyone but William Shakespeare could produce a play like *Madame Bovary* in three weeks flat. There was no time for revision. Hot from the typewriter, I would rush scene after scene in to Doris, who would have some extra copies made and start rehearsing them that night. Needless to say, it had its faults, and I got a thrashing in the press for having had the temerity to desecrate a masterpiece, while Doris was commended for her courage in playing the demanding part of Emma Bovary. No mention was made of the fact that she was uncertain of her lines, twenty years too old and many sizes too large. But that was Doris. She always liked to play the leading role and everyone applauded her.

Madame Bovary was soon forgotten when a fresh crisis occurred between Guido and myself. I had not seen very much of him while I was preoccupied with Alan Williamson; he had ceased coming to the house and I no longer went to Newport at weekends, as Gilda was now at boarding school. I had sworn that she would never suffer the pangs of homesickness as I had done during my early years at Oberwyl, but Lock Maree was altogether different. It was a fine old mansion in Vaucluse with extensive grounds and the water of Sydney Harbour lapping at its foot. Above all, it had Linda MacIntosh, a benign despot who looked upon her charges as her family. After the first interview with Linda, I no longer had any doubts about committing Gilda to her care.

She had been quite happy at Newport, and my reason for taking her away had nothing to do with my initial feeling of resentment at Ula having been her surrogate mother for the past two years. I had got over that completely, and the bond between us had been strengthened by our having accepted the fact that we were two women sharing a mutual love for one man. We had been welded into a family, dependent on each other and sharing the same interests.

An incurable romantic, that is how I saw myself, and was prepared to go on like that forever when a totally unforeseen fourth element insinuated itself and the peaceful trio was shattered forever.

The unforeseen element was a dim little woman who, ironically enough, lived in another part of Castlecrag. Her name was Ethel Cramp. I had seen her once at the bus stop on the corner of Edinburgh Road; she had a large cardboard folder under her arm and I guessed she was an artist of some kind. We exchanged a few casual words, and then the bus arrived and I thought no more about her. Now she was no longer a dim shadow in the background but a potent force that had transformed a rational being verging on old age into a man obsessed by a passion that would have done justice to a youth in his teens.

The effect on Ula was quite devastating. The painful rash that had tormented her while she and Guido had been living in the Cross came back and burned her skin like fire. I caught sight of her kneeling beside the bed one time, her face buried in her hands as she tried to muffle the groans she could not suppress. It was a pitiful sight, and I felt a wave of anger at the man who was inflicting so much anguish on a woman who had been unfortunate enough to fall in love with him.

Ula did not suffer alone. I developed shingles and had my own period of misery. Then came the night when we walked arm-in-arm along the road at Newport, united in our common woe. She was shaking violently and could barely articulate her words.

'If I had known the kind of pain that I was causing you, I would never have done it,' she said.

Every remaining particle of regard that I had felt for Guido was gone, and I saw him for the first time as the flawed man that he was.

'Guido Baracchi has left a trail of broken-hearted women and fatherless children behind him,' Justus Jorgensen had said. I had not been able to deny it at the time, and now the truth of it was confirmed.

We had a series of violent quarrels, in which Guido made no effort to defend himself. 'Betsy, I can't explain it. I just fell in love with her and it's something stronger than myself,' was all he said.

And I, who too had loved like that, not once but twice, could say no more. Nevertheless, the bitterness remained. I did not want to see him, and I felt I could not bear to witness Ula's misery.

That explains why Gilda was now a boarder at Loch Maree and I began to reconsider my decision to go and live at Montsalvat.

If I had told Freidel Fink about this he would have laughed and said: 'Betty, why do you keep on deceiving yourself? You're not angry with Guido because he's made Ula unhappy, it's because he's fallen in love with this other woman and hasn't come back to you.'

But I did not tell Friedel, as I no longer saw him. Neither did I see Lotte or Mona van Wein or Tommy Challon or any of the other habitués of the Cross. They belonged to another world, one that I wanted to forget. It had brought me no happiness, only a sense of failure and defeat. I had not fared much better after my return to Castlecrag, and the disastrous ending of the affair with Alan Williamson had increased my feeling of discouragement. Nothing lasted, everything seemed impermanent. My luck had deserted me from the moment I had set foot on Castlecrag. I would sell the house and leave the place forever. While Montsalvat and Jorgensen might not be the solution to my problem, it was a fresh start, and at least I could no longer delude myself that Guido was ever going to come back to me.

Aware of the gossip that was hissing up and down Edinburgh Road and the malicious eyes that marked Guido's passing as he went to visit Ethel Cramp, I had been even less inclined to have any contact with my neighbours than I had had before. Roberta was the sole exception. She had known about Alan Williamson from the first, had shared in my happiness at having found the man I was looking for, and had been appalled when the disaster fell. So when the day of departure came and I closed the door of the house behind me for the last time, she was the only one to see me go or have any idea that I was never coming back.

It was early February, the season of the rains, I had a long and lonely drive ahead of me and a future that was dark and insecure. Rain streamed down the windscreen and, although it was only early afternoon, I had turned the headlamps on. I was reminded of the time when I had driven through the storm from Lakes Entrance to Melbourne with a desperately sick child on the seat behind me, Peter, my son, who had died soon afterwards. The future had been dark indeed at that time, then Guido had come and brought hope and happiness.

Maybe there was another Guido waiting for me at Montsalvat. I had not yet ceased to hope.

CHAPTER 13

As the next two years are fully documented in a previous book, *The Eye of the Beholder*, there is no point in repeating the story here. Suffice it to say that I was not happy at Montsalvat, and at the end of the second year decided I was unsuited to communal life and moved into a house that I had bought on a sudden impulse after a heated debate between Jorgensen and myself. It was by no means the first occasion on which we had met head-on, and I had usually given way, but this time Gilda was involved and I was not prepared to have him dictate to me about where she should be sent to school.

For the past two years she had been going to a small local school with the other three Montsalvat children, Sebastian, Saskia, and Sigmund, but the time had come for them to move into a higher grade, and there the dispute began. Anxious that Gilda have nothing but the best, or what I thought to be the best, I had decided on a rather snobbish school called Tintern, while Seb, Sas, and Sig were to go to Eltham High.

'There must be no special privileges for your daughter here,' the Master had proclaimed. 'So, if she is to stay at Montsalvat with me [note the 'me'!], she must share the same conditions as the others.'

The argument, as usual, took place around the dinner table and grew heated; everybody had opinions but none of them supported me and when someone on whom I thought I could depend stood up and shouted: 'Why don't you use your brains and *think*, you silly bitch?', that was the end, and I walked out. A walk along a shady road is always a good idea if you want to cool your temper, and mine had scarcely begun to cool when I saw the house.

It was an unpretentious place, redeemed by its lovely garden.

I had often admired it, and had heard it was for sale, but until I saw the notice on the gate, no thought of buying it had occurred to me. Now I went in and asked the price. It was nothing excessive and well within my means—the house at Castlecrag could pay for it three times over—so I asked if I could have a look inside, saw its possibilities, and said that I would buy it, never dreaming what a bargain I had got.

As well as the lovely garden, there was a considerable amount of land below the house and what I thought to be a largish shed but proved to be another house, consisting of one large room, a kitchen and a veranda. It was partly hidden by some fruit trees and I had scarcely noticed it when I had made my purchase, but it was not long before I realised that by expending a few hundred pounds, I could add another room and a bathroom, and have a snug little cottage. This was eagerly snapped up by the mathematics teacher from Eltham High. He had a young wife, and it was exactly what they needed, as the rent was low.

The cheque from the *SMH* continued to make its regular appearance, I had the income from my Aunt Belle's estate and the rent from the cottage and felt that I was singularly fortunate. Admittedly I was still alone, but that was less disturbing than it had been before as I had grown accustomed to it. And if there were times when someone stayed the night, none was more than a temporary guest.

Montsalvat was only a short walk away, so Gilda still had the companionship of the three children there, rode their ponies, splashed with them in the swimming pool, and suffered no loss because of my sudden departure from the place. Nor did she seem to have suffered any ill effects from having been deprived of her father, who at this time was preparing to leave Ula and go to Europe with his new love, Ethel.

Tranquillity and I are never more than passing acquaintances, and this temporary calm in a stormy life was suddenly disturbed when Roberta sent a telegram saying she was coming down to see me. Poor Edgar had died since I had seen her last, and I had often wondered how she was coping with the responsibility of caring for three young children without his forbearance and support. Something told me that she was in some sort of crisis and that I was about to be involved.

She omitted to tell me when she would arrive, and I was away from the house when the taxi left her at the gate. With unerring instinct, she found her way to the local pub. It was mid-afternoon and the pub was full of thirsty men. Roberta was a marked success, and when she finally appeared, accompanied by two men in a delivery van, she was in what can only be described as 'high spirits'. There was a certain clash of opinions when she urged her escorts to accompany her inside, and it took some persuasion on my part to convince them that they would not be welcome. I think they had come in the expectation of a jolly foursome, and they were very much put out when these hopes were dashed. Eventually they left, and Roberta walked unsteadily along the path, through the door, and collapsed into a chair.

'Darling, I'm pregnant!' she announced, accompanied by peals of laughter.

I have to admit that there are times when I resemble my disapproving aunt, and this was one of them. The resemblance grew stronger when she told me who the second party was. I was too dumbfounded to speak. I had no reason to disbelieve her and it was too preposterous for even Roberta to invent. The man in the case was one of Sydney's pillars of the church, a man of the cloth of so much piety and unblemished reputation that even now, long after he has died, I dare not call him by name. She wept unrestrainedly for quite some time and begged for another drink. Aunt Belle-like, I refused and made her go to bed, gave her strong black coffee, and let her go to sleep.

Next day she was her usual self and gave me some details of the affair. They had set up a love-nest in a back lane in the city and there they had their orgies in the afternoon.

'He said he would like to fuck me so hard that it would come out my mouth,' she said triumphantly.

Finally, I learned the real purpose of her visit. I had written to her when Edgar died and enclosed a photo of my new house and the cottage in the garden. In her reply she said she thought that it looked charming and wished that she could come and live in it, which was precisely what she now proposed to do! She had decided to have the baby and would live in the cottage, knit baby clothes, and think beautiful thoughts until it arrived.

Aunt Belle would have been proud of me had she heard my response to this astounding proposition. Poor Roberta wilted under the tirade that descended onto her.

What did she propose to do with Michael and Nicky and Mary while this fairytale took place? She hadn't thought of that. Was the reverend gentleman prepared to support her and the child? She thought he would, but wasn't sure.

It occurred to me that she had a rare opportunity for blackmail, but I put the thought aside; Roberta was not the type. In the end, I bullied her into going back to Sydney and having an abortion, no novelty to her as, to my knowledge, she had already had three. So, calm but resigned, she said goodbye and did as I had said.

But Roberta had not finished with me yet. A few months had elapsed when a letter arrived announcing her intention to go to Paris and visit Michael. It appeared that she had become friendly with the wife of the Canadian consul and had persuaded her to take the boy with her when her husband had received the Paris posting. Michael was then twelve years old and still suffered from asthma, but wanted to be a ballet dancer, so Paris seemed a good place in which to practise arabesques. It also relieved Roberta of one of her responsibilities. Michael's legs had proved unequal to the strain, however, and his hostess was starting to regret her generosity. Would I have Nicky to come and stay with me while she was away?

Nicky! The wild little creature that had refused to be petted when he was a baby, who was intent on leaving home as soon as he could walk and had to be fastened to a tree with a rope around his waist—was I to have him come and live with me and totally disrupt my life? Rebel though he was, I had always

116

liked his independence, his bright mind, and the charm he had inherited from his mother. Also I had always wanted another child, a boy for preference, and here was one ready-made, and no ordinary child either, so I wrote to say that I would be pleased to have him.

But only under certain conditions. During her absence, I was to have complete control of Nicky's life. I would be responsible for his maintenance but must be empowered to negotiate the terms of any contract for film, radio, or stage performances, the money for which would be paid into a trust account in his name. Roberta agreed, and not long afterwards Nicky and his dog arrived. Roberta had pleaded that the dog be included in the deal.

His father's death had been a heavy blow to Nick. Neither his mother nor his half-brother, Michael, nor the little love-child, Mary, had counted for very much with him, but Edgar was his hero and the one person who had never failed him. Now this mainstay of his life was gone and the little dog, Bamby, had brought a degree of comfort. Nicky loved him dearly.

I met them at the airport. The car had what was known as a 'sunshine' roof and Nick insisted on standing upright on the front seat, his head protruding through the open roof, long hair flying in the wind, and Bamby dribbled saliva down my back. I had a Siamese cat who took one look at Bamby and was not seen again for several days. In spite of this rather inauspicious beginning, the new regime worked out quite well. Underneath his wild exterior, Nick was a sweet-natured child, and after recovering from his initial resentment at being bossed about by a woman, settled in quite happily and went off to school with Gilda and Seb and Sas and Sig from Montsalvat. He made friends with a boy called Gavin Bowie, and the pair spent a great deal of their time together, which led to a minor crisis that might have been a disaster.

I rarely went into town at night but had made an exception when a celebrated author came out from England and was being fêted at a dinner held in the Menzies Hotel. The first course had been served when a waiter touched me on the shoulder and

117

said that a message had come for me to say that Nick had met with an accident and would I please come home. The dinner was forgotten and I never knew what the famous man said in his after-dinner speech, but broke all the regulations in the drive back to Eltham to find Nicky sitting up in bed, his face rather pale and a nose that was squashed completely flat!

He and Gavin had found a boomerang and tried their skill by hurling this ancient weapon of the Aborigines across a paddock near the house. It had circled back as it was supposed to do and struck Nick just below his eyes.

A broken nose was nothing compared to the disaster that it could have caused, but Nicky Yardley's nose was no ordinary nose: it was attached to a boy whose future as a film star could well depend on its shape, and one for whom I had demanded full responsibility. So on the following day I took him down to Melbourne and, by the exercise of much persuasion and a degree of personality, managed to get an appointment with the leading plastic surgeon in Collins Street. The appointment was not until late in the afternoon, so we had lunch and I remember watching Nick devour a plate of sausages and chips with a malted milk to follow.

The surgeon, whose name I cannot recall, was not very pleased to see us, nor was he impressed when I told him the importance of restoring Nicky's nose to its original shape.

'I don't usually do cosmetic surgery,' he told me loftily, but after further entreaties on my part, he reluctantly agreed, adding that the reshaping had already been delayed too long and he must operate at once. So arrangements were made for Nick to be admitted to the Heidelberg hospital and, having delivered him there, I hurried back to Eltham, got a pair of Nick's pyjamas and his toothbrush and went back to Heidelberg.

I found him resting in a private ward, a plaster mask across his face and a pair of the blackest eyes ever seen outside the boxing ring. Oddly enough, he was not in any pain, nor had he been since the accident occurred.

The nurse on duty met me with a disapproving look. 'What

did you give him for lunch?' she asked. 'Don't you know it's highly dangerous to eat solid food before an operation?'

I did know, but had not realised that Nick would be hustled into the operating theatre at such short notice. Apparently he had been violently sick while under the anaesthetic and had given everyone a fright. He was discharged from hospital after the second day, and they were not sorry to see him go, as he had amused himself by hurling paper darts at the passers-by from the balcony of his room. The nose was fully restored, however, and his eyes soon resumed their former shape.

Despite my concern about his nose, Nick's career as an actor did not progress beyond this point. I did nothing to promote it— rightly or wrongly, I felt that he was in need of a little less attention and should be allowed to lead the life of an ordinary child. Had there been directors clamouring for his services I might have felt otherwise, but his reputation had not followed him from Sydney. Nobody in Melbourne was aware that the star of *Bush Christmas* was among them, and I made no attempt to tell them. Perhaps another Peter Finch was lost, but I did what I thought was best for Nick, and the life of an actor, even a Peter Finch, is not so rosy that anyone should envy him.

When Nick was seven and playing TylTyl in *The Bluebird*, he had attracted the attention of a certain Professor Giblin, who, having no children of his own, took a keen interest in other people's. Nick won a special place in his heart and he became a sort of deputy grandfather to the engaging little boy, kept a watchful eye on him, and, I have no doubt, contributed to his upkeep after Edgar died. Roberta had spoken of him in glowing terms, so I was pleased when he wrote to say he would be passing through Melbourne on his way home from Canberra—his permanent home was in Hobart—and would like to visit us in Eltham. I found him to be a gentle, humorous and lovable old man, whose unassuming manner belied his reputation as an economist of world stature and a distinguished man of letters. He and Nick had two happy days together, and before he left he talked to me about Nick's future.

He did not need to be told that I had taken on an enormous responsibility and that there were times when I wondered how long I could continue to cope. Nick was now twelve years old and outgrew his clothes at an alarming rate. There was also the matter of his education. Like Gilda and the three at Montsalvat, he had progressed beyond the local school and must go somewhere else. Gilda was to go to Tintern in the new year, but what was to be done with Nick? There was Eltham High, of course, and it seemed he must go there, but Giblin had other ideas. He had been making enquiries and had found that Ivanhoe Grammar had an excellent reputation and suggested that Nick should go there, not as a day boy but as a boarder, and at his expense.

I cannot pretend that this was not an enormous relief, as I had recently received a letter from the editor of the *SMH* informing me that he had reluctantly decided to dispense with *The Conways*—it cost too much and a syndicated strip could be had for half the price, from America of course. Consequently I was once more faced with the uncertainties of working as a freelance writer. But my luck—or was it Jupiter?—had not completely deserted me. I sent an appeal to my friend, Nell Stirling, and she wrote back to say she was in need of a daytime serial with a strong appeal to women. So I cooked up a story about a woman whose husband was unfaithful to her—it was called *A Woman Scorned*—and got busy thinking up ways in which she could make the cad regret his infidelity. It had the ring of truth, was a big success and drew top ratings when it went to air.

I had had five years of earning easy money with time to spare for better things. Perhaps I had failed to take advantage of my opportunity, but I had been preoccupied with the business of living and had learnt many things, so it was not entirely wasted. Also, I had taken out the play that had defeated me before and worked on it again, and felt it was not an unworthy successor to *The Touch of Silk*. It now had a central theme and a bite, whereas it had been flabby and weak in its original version. When the Commonwealth Government announced it would award a prize of five hundred pounds for a three-act play as part of its

Jubilee celebrations, *Granite Peak* was among the seventy plays submitted, and I felt there was a good chance that it would win the prize. The judges decided otherwise, however, and a play called *Tether a Dragon*, by Kylie Tennant, received the award instead.

It is possible that Kylie needed the five hundred pounds far more than I did, but she did not need the boost to her reputation as a writer in the way that I did. I was filled with disgust at the rubbish I had been churning out. Top ratings did not impress me in the least, they merely indicated the lack of taste on the part of the people who listened. I wanted to be recognised as a serious playwright, and had hoped that, by winning the award for *Granite Peak*, I might be restored to the position I had occupied in 1928. Had the critic on the *Bulletin* not hailed me as 'Australia's first genuine playwright'?

Disappointment turned to indignation when I read Kylie's play. It reminded me of the *Madame Bovary* play in its initial form—a mishmash of scenes and characters. What made it worse, it was about Henry Parkes, a pompous old politician, not a beautiful woman who loved unwisely and met with a tragic fate and was never a crashing bore.

That *Granite Peak* should be judged inferior to this non-play seemed like a personal insult, and my anger mounted steadily. I had given Australia two good plays. One had been forgotten, the other had been ignored and, so far as I was concerned, that was the end. I would never write another play again. I would leave Australia to the Philistines and seek recognition overseas.

I was then close to fifty years of age. How much time did I have left? I asked myself. Thirty years, at the most. Perhaps it was already too late to start another life, but I still looked young enough to pass for thirty-five. To hell with everything and everyone—I was going to try my luck in London.

The euphoria of the postwar years had not yet subsided and there was a rush of Australians to Europe that resembled a stampede. Air travel had not advanced beyond the experimental stage, and the boats that went via Suez or Cape Town were crowded to capacity, so it was necessary to book several months ahead in order to secure a berth. I went to the Flotto Lauro shipping company and booked a two-berth cabin on the *Marco Polo*, which was due to sail in February 1952. It was then September 1951, which gave me ample time to simmer down and consider the consequences of the decision I had made.

First and foremost, there was Gilda. She was then fourteen and had reached the critical stage of puberty. How would she react to this new disruption to her life? There was no question whatever as to whether or not she should come with me—the only alternative would be to send her back to Ula, which was quite unthinkable. Fourteen was a good age at which to be introduced to the marvels of Europe; she was old enough to appreciate them, yet young enough to adjust herself to a totally different world. She would go to school in England, make new friends, and acquire an English accent. The advantages would heavily outweigh the disadvantages, so I convinced myself.

There still remained the question of what to do about Nick. He had been at Ivanhoe Grammar for more than a year and appeared to be quite happy there, though there had been a painful period when dear old Professor Giblin had died. Perhaps he had known that the end was not far off when he came to stay with us, but the telegram that came from his wife and said: 'Lyn died peacefully last night' was a stunning blow and gave me the painful task of telling poor Nick that, for the second time in his short life, death had deprived him of the being he loved best.

He took it manfully. He shed no tears and barely said a word, but his face went very white and the set expression round his mouth told me that the blow had hit him very hard. He shook his head when I asked if he would like to come back to Eltham with me, and I stifled an impulse to take him in my arms, remembering how he had resisted Roberta when she had tried to embrace him as a baby. Before I left I had asked to see his housemaster, James Murray, and told him what had happened. James promised to keep a watchful eye on Nick, especially that night when the lights in the dormitory were out and he would be alone with his grief. James kept his word, and a bond of affection between man and boy was forged in those lonely hours, a bond that lasted until Nick grew up and his restless spirit took him wandering around the world.

Giblin, the good old man, had left sufficient money in a trust fund to pay Nick's fees at Ivanhoe Grammar and take him to the university if he chose an academic career. This assured his immediate future but what was to become of him when I went away? Roberta appeared to have forgotten him, she was still in London and wrote to say she had met a white Russian living there and planned to marry him. Then James Murray said that his parents who lived in Hawthorn would be happy to have Nick come and live with them. So Nick had a home, James assumed the role of elder brother, and my conscience was at rest.

CHAPTER 14

Kylie Tennant's play was not the only reason I had for leaving Australia. There was a second and even more urgent one for making the decision: I had fallen quite desperately in love with a married man.

It happened during the wine festival in the Barossa Valley, which was as likely a time and place for such a thing to happen as can be imagined. The Barossa is always a place of great beauty and charm but during the annual festival it surrenders itself to the celebration of Bacchus and the worship of the vine. I was there to write an account of events for a women's magazine and was the guest of one of the many vignerons whose ancestors had come from Silesia a century ago and brought cuttings of their choicest vines with them.

There was the mandatory barbecue one night, and through the aroma of lamb roasting on a spit and the soft glow of burning logs, I saw a pair of dark eyes staring at me through the smoke. Ever since the time when Nick, the soldier in B Company, had marched into my life, brown eyes had had a strong effect on me. A chance encounter in the street, a casual glance when passing through a door, would cause a sudden quickening of the pulse and tell me I had not forgotten him. Now, here was his double, standing in the firelight as Nick had done and with the same demand in his eyes.

It was a tempestuous affair, only this time there was a wife and not a woman in Woolloomooloo in the background and a little girl of three whose father was besotted with her. There was an older boy as well, who did not constitute an obstacle— his father spoke of him with some distaste. The marriage, it appeared, was none too sound, but it had survived the separation of the war years and would probably endure as long as someone like myself did not intervene. Which placed me in the anomalous position Ula had occupied with regard to Guido and myself.

I had hated and despised her then, had sworn that I would never be guilty of the crime of destroying a marriage and inflicting on another woman the pain that I had suffered at the time. I had called her a moral thief, and had remained unmoved when Guido had said that his love for Ethel Cramp was something that was stronger than himself. Now I was being called to account and must show if I had merely paid lip-service to high principles or was no better than the two I had condemned.

I cannot claim any great virtue for having booked that cabin on the *Marco Polo*; it was more a matter of sound common-sense than superior moral standards. I had learnt a lot in the past few years and could sense disaster were I to obey my inclination and not put myself beyond the reach of all temptation. The wife was certain to learn the truth of her husband's intermittent absences and could sue for divorce—she might even be glad of an opportunity to do so—and to be involved in another scandal, especially in Melbourne, was a thing I did not care to contemplate.

Gilda had been largely unaware of my past irregularities but she was too old now to remain in ignorance of what took place this time and would certainly suffer from the repercussions of a divorce. There had been talk of the man going with me, but the effect on her could be even worse. He was a demanding man and she might be made to feel she was unwanted for the first time in her life. That, in the early years of adolescence and in a strange environment, could have a disastrous effect. The voice of Friedel Fink rang loudly in my ears. Lastly, there was the little girl. There was no way that she could go with her father. The law prohibited a minor from being taken out of the country without parental consent and what mother would agree to her child being taken to London by a father who had forfeited all right to her? There was only one way in which to solve the dilemma and by reserving a cabin on the *Marco Polo* I felt that I had taken it.

If I am ever troubled by a feeling of unrest and think about

126

returning to the Europe that I learned to love so much, all I need to do is recall the traumas that inevitably accompany such departures, and the impulse dies. The departure of January 1952 stands out in my memory as one of unmitigated hell. When I had gone away with Guido it had only been a matter of packing up my clothes, disposing of some books, and boarding the SS *Ballarat* with the minimum of fuss. This time there was a house to sell, furniture and effects to be disposed of, passports and permits to be obtained, the after effects of smallpox, cholera and typhoid vaccines to be endured, bank drafts, traveller's cheques, letters of introduction, tax clearances, electric light bills, water rates, paper bills, charge accounts to be closed, more bills, farewell parties—all the inescapable, time-consuming and exhausting details to be attended to and no-one but myself to do them. How I longed for a man, just any man, to relieve me of some of them.

An unexpected hitch occurred when I went into the Flotto Lauro Shipping Company to collect my ticket. The *Marco Polo* was due to sail in a month's time, but I had received no request to pay the balance of the fare to Genoa. The clerk in the office took out the passenger list and read it carefully, then he went back and read it through again. Then he held a consultation with another clerk, while I began to grow alarmed. Finally, they both confronted me. White-faced and apologetic, they had to admit that a grave error had been made—my name had been omitted from the list. No cabin had been reserved for me and, alas, the *Marco Polo* was full to capacity.

It was a situation that called for histrionics and hysteria and I made the most of it. I had sold my house and all my choice possessions in the belief that the company could be relied upon. I and my child were homeless, we had nowhere to go, a poor lone woman who had put her trust in them. It was a virtuoso performance, and it got results. After another hasty consultation, more searching of passenger lists, I was told that there was a cabin on the *Cyrenia*, a Greek ship due to sail at the same time as the *Marco Polo* and which they could thoroughly recommend.

A Greek ship! The mere suggestion was an outrage as the

Cyrenia had recently been the subject of much unfavourable publicity in the daily press, which had reported complaints of unsanitary conditions, overcrowding, dysentery and cockroaches.

'Ah, but only on the outward voyage', was the suave reply. 'Then it is full of migrants. Homeward bound it is a different story altogether. We can offer you a two-berth cabin on the promenade deck, with toilet and bath en suite, and the fare will be a third less than on the *Marco Polo.*'

I said I would think the matter over, and went home. The idea of saving several hundred pounds was a tempting one, and there was also the thought of Greece. Why not leave the *Cyrenia* when she reached Piraeus and continue our journey to Genoa on another ship? The money saved would give us a month in the land of the heroes and the gods. The thought was irresistible, and the *Cyrenia*, however bad, would be tolerable if, at the end of an unpleasant voyage, the Acropolis, Delphi, Sounion, and Mycenae awaited us.

I went back to the Flotto Lauro. Yes, it could be arranged. All that was needed was an endorsement on my passport. I had better attend to that right away, I was told, as Christmas was approaching and the consul might not be available. The consul was not available; he was only an honorary consul and took his duties lightly so had already gone off to Sydney for a month's vacation. Suppose he changed his mind and did not come back before the *Cyrenia* sailed? I asked. The girl in the office acknowledged that this was not impossible and suggested that the passports, Gilda's and mine, be sent to Sydney to be endorsed and returned by registered post. It was a decided risk, as Christmas mail was notoriously unreliable, but my heart was set on that month in Greece, and I took the risk.

Christmas came and went, the new owner took possession of the house, farewells were made, and Gilda and I moved into the temporary flat in East Melbourne in which we were to spend the final days—and I began to clamour for the passports, which had not been returned. The girl at the consul's office was vague about his whereabouts. Telegrams were sent and I grew more frantic as day after day went past. The trauma was increased when I learned that unless I produced my passport the Flotto Lauro line could not issue me a ticket. The reason was not clear, but that was the company's rule and it had to be observed.

Then came the final day and the girl in the consul's office rang to say the passports had arrived. The *Cyrenia* was due to sail at half-past two. Some friends had planned a farewell lunch at Mario's, but I had a large trunk and some smaller pieces of luggage that must be taken to the wharf at Williamstown before I could collect the passports. There was the usual delay at the customs shed and it was after eleven o'clock by the time I had dealt with that. Seizing Gilda by the hand, I made a dash to the consul's office. A different girl was there from the one I had seen before, and that meant some delay, but finally I had the passports in my hand. Next, to the shipping company. It was now close to one o'clock, and all thought of the farewell lunch had been dismissed. Furthermore, there was a queue in the Flotto Lauro office that appeared to be incapable of motion. Finally it was my turn, but the tickets could not be found. After a frantic search, they were discovered under the name of 'Rowland' instead of the more unusual Roland, a mistake that often occurred. Meanwhile, the hands of the clock moved on.

'Number three wharf,' I gasped to the taxi driver. It was a scorching day; Gilda's face was white and mine was as red as beetroot. Neither of us was capable of speech. The taxi stopped, I paid the fare and hurried onto the wharf. There was no sign of the *Cyrenia*, the place was silent and deserted and I realised we were not at Williamstown but somewhere else, *where* I did not know. I thought that I would faint.

'Quick! Let's see if we can catch that taxi!' Grabbing Gilda's hand, I dragged her back onto the road, catching the heel of my shoe in a crack as I went. The heel came off and I picked it up and continued to hobble along. There was no sign of the taxi anywhere or anything else that moved. There are moments so bleak that all thoughts and feelings are suspended, and this was one of them. I did not know where we were, the *Cyrenia* was about to sail, and there was no way of reaching her before she did.

Then, like a figment of the imagination, a taxi came round the corner and two men got out. It was some distance away but I managed to attract their attention. My mouth was so dry I could scarcely speak to say what happened.

'*Cyrenia*,' the driver said. 'I know where she is. Hop in.'

I have no recollection whatever of the drive, but it wasn't very long, and soon, with the broken heel still in one hand, Gilda clinging to the other, I staggered onto the wharf. The gangway had started to rise but was lowered when we appeared, hands helped us scramble aboard, the second mate murmured a few words of reproach at us for having caused a delay, and the *Cyrenia* cast off and started to move away.

It took a while to recover my breath or even be aware that Williamstown, and Melbourne too, were rapidly slipping away from me and into the past. In order to take a final look, I went to the rail and looked down. There on the deserted wharf was the cabin trunk and the three smaller pieces of luggage that I had totally forgotten.

But this story has a happy ending. Once the *Cyrenia* had been safely navigated through the treacherous channels between the twin headlands of Port Phillip Bay, a launch came out to collect the pilot and take him back to base. It had the trunk and its companion pieces on its deck and, with a feeling of unspeakable relief, I saw them put into a sling and hoisted on board.

During the turmoil of the final weeks there had been little time to brood over the Barossa Valley man, but in the lazy days and nights in mid-ocean he was constantly in my thoughts. There was little to distract them. Besides Gilda and myself, there were only five other passengers, and none of them were what could be termed exciting. There was a Greek couple who had made a lot of money in Australia and were going back to their island village in the Aegean in order to amaze their relatives with stories of the modern Eldorado; a young man going on a pilgrimage

130

to Mount Athos, and a middle-aged man from Derbyshire and his companion, a rather toothy woman who had bad breath. They had hired a car and travelled for thousands of miles through the backblocks of Australia and the chief impressions they took away with them were of bad hotels, red dust and bush flies.

The voyage promised to be tedious, but the cabin in which a large part of my time was spent was everything the shipping clerk had promised it would be. It was on the promenade deck, on the side that did not get the afternoon sun, was roomy, had beds instead of bunks, and a bathroom with shower and all amenities. Then there were the meals! Greek food, provided it is the work of an expert, can be truly *haute cuisine* and the chef on the *Cyrenia* was a master of his craft. Lack of convivial companions meant that there was plenty of time to lean across the rail on the top deck, watching the bow-wave break in a smother of foam, remembering two dark eyes seen through a veil of smoke.

The eyes of the man in Massawa, however, were blue.

Massawa is a barren, heat-blistered port on the Red Sea, and struck me as a good place to avoid. Even when the sun went down the heat made sleep impossible and the rattle and bang of the winches as the holds were relieved of their cargo and fresh bales and crates put in their place did nothing to relieve the tedium and discomfort.

Gilda had managed to sleep and there was nobody on deck, so I went down to the saloon in search of a cool drink. There was a steward behind the bar and a man perched on a stool with a long drink of something at his elbow. He had a military look and was wearing the regulation khaki shorts, safari jacket, brown shoes and knee-high socks. I cannot remember his name; perhaps he told me what it was, but it is of little consequence. He was stationed in this godforsaken place and had come on board the *Cyrenia* in the hope of finding someone who would help relieve his sense of isolation and chronic boredom.

He brightened when I came through the door and asked me would I like to have a drink. It was the classic approach and I responded in kind. It happened a long time ago, and what the next move was I do not know, but I have a clear recollection of standing on a bare patch of earth with the impenetrable darkness of Africa around me and thinking, 'This is Africa. You're standing on Africa,' and feeling a faint sensation on my skin, as though invisible ants were crawling over it.

Another clear recollection is of a sort of watchtower on a headland on the outskirts of the town, and a stark room furnished with a bed, a table and a chair. I suppose I had been driven there in a jeep, I do not know, but can vaguely remember passing a building where there were lights and the sound of bongo drums and people singing. I had asked to be taken inside to see, but had been told that it was no place for a white woman to go and I said no more.

The Red Sea is not noted for its turbulence, but there were waves that washed around the cliff below the tower. They made a languid, unhurried background to the lovemaking that took place. It was voluptuous and slow and met a need that both of us shared. Who he was and what he was doing in that desolate port in Eritrea, I do not know, but the memory remains of those somnolent waves and the heat of an African night.

CHAPTER 15

Shortly before we reached Piraeus the cabin steward asked me would I take a package ashore for him. I was doubtful at first but after questioning him about its contents, said that I would. He was a pleasant and polite young man, but that was no guarantee that he would not make use of me to smuggle contraband ashore, but as it turned out all he wanted to do was avoid having to pay heavy duty on the coffee set that he had bought in Aden. I reassured myself on this by opening the package and taking a look. I have a strong instinct for self-preservation and did not want to start breaking the law the first moment I set foot in Greece. It was a small thing to do and I was amply repaid.

The moment we stepped onto the Piraeus wharf we were surrounded by a clamouring mob of porters, would-be interpreters, touts and taxi drivers, all desperate to earn the few odd drachmas their services would receive. It was a frenzied scene unknown in Australia, and Gilda grew alarmed, clutched my hand and drew close to my side. Help arrived in the shape of the cabin steward, who thrust himself through the melée, shouted a few words in Greek and got immediate results. He was followed by another young man who he said was his brother and would be pleased to help us through customs and accompany us to Athens. I don't for a moment imagine that he was also there to keep an eye on the packet containing the coffee service. There was no trouble from the customs officer; we were waved through the checkpoint without a glance at any of our possessions, and with a minimum of fuss were in a taxi and on our way to Athens.

Conversation was limited, as our new friend knew little English, but even what there was broke off when the unbelievable perfection of the Parthenon appeared in the blue brilliance of the sky. A first glimpse of the Parthenon is surely one of the great moments in life, and for that moment I had travelled all those long sea miles, abandoned friends, security and home. Breathless, unable to speak for the wonder of it all, I felt that the price had not been one penny too much to pay. Five minutes more, and we were in the heart of Athens.

Athens, in the year 1952, was a gentle, shabby little city still scarred by the wounds of recent wars. It is now a great metropolis, and tall skyscrapers shut away the sight of the Acropolis which was once visible from every quarter of the town, and the mellow tiles of ancient roofs, the harmony of old stone walls—sagging, lichen-covered—have been replaced by concrete and the austere elegance of chromium and glass. But it was still a place of poetry in 1952, and our companion pointed to the shattered buildings and shrapnel-pitted walls that were the legacy of World War II and the disastrous civil war that had followed in its wake.

It was this succession of disasters that had reduced the country to the point of ruin and its currency to lunatic levels that were to throw me into a panic until I grasped the fact that a million drachmas amounted to a mere one hundred English pounds; by knocking a few zeros off the end of a bill, one's sanity was preserved. But no such simple equation occurred to me when I stood at the reception desk of the Grande Bretagne Hotel and enquired the price of a room.

The Grande Bretagne, known affectionately as the GB, is a splendid structure that has survived all wars and revolutions and appears to be frequented by foreign diplomats, millionaires and film stars, so it was by sheer mischance that I ever got inside its doors at all. This arose from the fact that in 1952, as now, all Greeks cherished the belief that foreign visitors possessed unlimited wealth and were ready, even eager, to pay large sums for the simplest commodity. Accordingly, the kind young man now in possession of the coffee set had told the taxi driver to take us to this splendid hostelry.

The man at the reception desk betrayed no interest at my diffident enquiry as to the price of a room but wrote some figures on a scrap of paper and handed it to me. There was a moment's stricken silence, then I feebly remarked that I thought I should try to find a hotel that was just a little less expensive. I carried that scrap of paper round with me for years, then it was lost, but I still remember that staggering total. It amounted to 62 500 drachmas for one night, heating and breakfast not included. I later learned that this was only £6 15s, but even that was far beyond my means.

The kind young man in the taxi was sympathetic and adjusted his ideas about my affluence and took us to a modest little building diagonally across the square from the Grande Bretagne. It was the Hotel New Angleterre, as nice a little place as one could wish to find. Its walls were shabby and its shutters badly needed paint, it had no mossy carpets on its scrubbed wooden floors, and the lift that took us to the second storey shook and grumbled and could scarcely make the grade. But the room we had was large and bright, with mid-Victorian furniture and two balconies which had, I am convinced, the most spectacular views in Athens.

From one we looked directly onto Syntagma Square, the Royal Palace and the Tomb of the Unknown Warrior, where two *evzones* in their long white stockings, pompoms on their shoes, white kilts and red jackets swaggered up and down. In the square were orange trees and myrtle flanked by flower beds, and dozens of iron chairs and little tables. Here the citizens of Athens sat and read their papers, gossiped and talked politics, drinking ouzo or the thick, sweet coffee that they dote on.

It could be said that from that balcony one looked into the heart of Athens, but from the other one saw its soul. Every morning when I threw aside the shutters, I looked across the rooftops and saw the Parthenon suspended in the sky. At night, it was the last thing that I saw, mysterious and ghostly, dimly lit by the stars and, for a few enchanted nights, the moon. And never did I look without a quickened pulse.

All this, and heat and breakfast too, for a mere £1 7s 6d a day. For lunch we bought sausage, sweet crisp bread, tomatoes, cheese and wine, and in the evening we climbed the endless steps that took us to the Plaka, the most ancient quarter of the town, where the aroma of souvlaki (goat's meat grilling over charcoal) and the music of the *bouzouki* would lure us into one of the dark little tavernas where we would sit and feast for an hour or so, and then walk wearily back to the New Angleterre.

Dear old New Angleterre! Like so many other things in Athens, it has vanished now. Progress, and American aid, have swept it away and a brash new office block built for American Express stands where its shabby walls and faded shutters blended gently into a background of old houses and outmoded shops. We had four enchanted weeks there, exploring Athens, taking a bus to Delphi, Epidaurus, Corinth, Sounion, Mycenae, Tiryns and Nauplion.

In the light of greater experience, I marvel at my temerity in setting out the way I did, knowing not a word of Greek, my child held firmly by the hand, with nothing but a naive faith in human nature, belief in my own luck, and starry-eyed wonder at finding myself in the very myth and mystery of Homer's Greece. The names of the ancient heroes were as familiar to me as those in the Old Testament: Hector, Jason, Agamemnon and Achilles, with Odysseus best loved of all.

We spent a day at Eleusis and sat with our backs against the Temple of Demeter and Gilda learned the legend of Persephone and Pluto. Together, we crossed the Isthmus of Corinth and wondered where it was that Theseus had slain Sinis, killed the man-devouring boar and after that the monstrous Sciron, then continued on his way to Athens and the fateful rendezvous in Crete with Ariadne and the Minotaur.

There was also Delphi, high, austere, remote in its mountain fastness. There was no-one there but ourselves, silence in the sacred olive groves, no footfall but our own in the deserted temples. One night, when Gilda was asleep, I stole out from the little inn and walked along the road with Parnassos sheer and stark above me in the moonlight. The night was so still and silent that the little stream, Castillia itself, that cascaded from the rocks and down the mountainside, seemed to hold the ripple of dryad voices and the gurgle of their laughter.

It was a night when Pan might well be lurking in the shadows, and when a great black dog came trotting down the road, he startled me so that I drew aside to let him pass. He cast a swift, suspicious look at me, then went about his secret business, vanishing into the night.

Delphi, so I have been told, is like Athens now, and has changed beyond all recognition, so that there is no longer any mystery at night. The one small inn in which we slept has been replaced by a dozen new hotels, and you have to fight your way along the Sacré Via, and the pestilence of the transistor radio has stilled the music of Castillia more effectively than any curse that fell upon Apollo's shrine. I never went back to see, nor could I ever bring myself to go back to Mycenae.

How could one ever recapture the magic of the evening when the bus drew up and a solitary woman and a child got out, stood hesitating as it disappeared along the road, looked at the signpost with the faded word 'MYCENAE' painted on its sagging arm, then set off along the track, rucksack slung between them on a stick, and a few Greek phrases on a piece of paper the sole means of asking the way.

I remember that it was then that I experienced my first faint sense of apprehension, an awareness of possible risks. Gilda, as always, was wide-eyed and silent; she was still bewildered by the sudden transition from familiar things to the unknown, and I felt suddenly vulnerable and alone.

There was total silence, no sign of any living thing, the sun was sinking rapidly behind the mountains, and there was already a hint of darkness under the trees. Then I saw that the trees were old familiar friends: an avenue of sturdy Australian eucalypts. Almost immediately, a burst of sunlight broke through the clouds, flooding the world with a warm wash of gold, and apprehension vanished.

Then the silence was broken by the sound of tiny bells and the reedy music of a pipe somewhere ahead of us. Rounding a bend in the road, we came upon a shepherd leading his flock of black and brown-fleeced sheep. His piping stopped at the sight of us and he stared in astonishment, then broke into a torrent of Greek.

All I could do was smile and spread my hands apologetically, unable to understand or tell him who I was or where I wanted to go. He clucked his tongue and wagged his head and put a knotted hand on Gilda's shoulder, admired her wild-rose colouring and long brown plaits, while the patient sheep stood still and waited for him to have done with sociability and lead them safely to the fold.

Across the unbridgeable gulf of our different tongues we did what we could to establish contact. I gave him cigarettes and took his photograph, and he, in the manner of all Greeks, was happy to pose among his sheep and wrote his name and address on a piece of paper so that I could send him back a print. Then we shook hands and said *hieretay* and he continued on his way, his tattered coat flapping around his knees, his grizzled head bound up in the inevitable handkerchief, his sheep at his heels. The fragile music of his pipe and the tinkle of sheep-bells lingered in our ears long after he had disappeared from sight.

There was no longer any sense of apprehension after that. A few minutes later we met some women riding home on donkeys. Their shrill chatter died when they saw us and I had an impression of weatherbeaten faces under bright scarves and of interested eyes that held a hint of disapproval. What was I doing there without a man? But this was dissipated by a smile, a wave of the hand and a word of greeting. They answered with a flash of strong white teeth and a chorus of Greek voices.

I know now that they called out '*Chaireté*' (greetings), or perhaps '*Kalos orissetay*' (you are welcome). But then I spoke no Greek, so all I knew was that there was friendliness around me and no longer any need to feel afraid. I showed them the slip of paper which told them where I wanted to go, and with one accord they turned their donkeys round and started to show me the way. We crossed a railway line and soon we saw the first stone houses of the village. Word of our coming seemed to have preceded us, as we were met by a party of women, children and dogs, who clustered round us, talking and questioning, laughing at our vain attempts to make ourselves understood, passing the scrap of paper from hand to hand and then leading us in a sort of triumphant procession to La Belle Hélène.

La Belle Hélène de Menelaeus is now so well known to so many thousands that it seems superfluous for me to write about it, but in 1952 I had never heard of it and could not conceal my delight at finding anything so improbable as a modest little inn with such a name in such a place as Mycenae. Nor did the enchantment end with this: our host, who hurried out to welcome us, was called Agamemnon, and he had a brother called Orestes. After this, it seemed in no way improbable that the guide who led us through the ruins of Mycenae should bear the name of Aristotle.

That night, however, it was Agamemnon who played host to us, serving thick soup and an omelette, dark peasant bread and salty goat's milk cheese called *feta*, with a bottle of retsina. A tribe of little boys came round us selling postcards until Agamemnon shooed them angrily away. Then he produced the visitor's book and we added our names to the list of travellers who had come from many corners of the world. With pardonable pride, he took down a framed letter that was hanging on the wall, and we saw that it was signed 'Field-Marshall Lord Alexander', thanking him for the part he had played in assisting some allied soldier to escape in the defeat of 1941 and commending him for his bravery. One of Agamemnon's legs was shorter than the other, a legacy from that time.

Then, seeing that we were sleepy, one of his daughters, beautiful and shapely as an Argive girl should be, led the way upstairs to a stark little room with two iron beds and a candle flickering on the windowsill. The night was frosty and bitterly cold, so Gilda and I were glad to creep into one of the beds together, draw the coarse dark blankets made of goats' hair up around our ears and fall asleep.

The following day was dazzlingly clear and we breakfasted outside with the snow-capped peaks of the Malevo mountains shining in the distance, the plains of Argos shimmering in the sunlight, and ate freshly baked bread, and honey gathered by bees that had sipped wild lavender and rosemary, cyclamen and crocus, and pale, ghostly asphodel.

Young Orestes passed by, leading his donkey off to gather cuttings from the olive groves, whistling as he went along the road, the pretty daughter shook a mat out of the window above our heads, while Agamemnon limped in and out on his twisted leg and made certain that the coffee was hot and the honey jar well filled.

Aristotle, meanwhile, sat sunning himself on a rock beside the road, waiting for us to finish our meal and begin our morning's expedition to the ruins. He led us along a winding track between the hills, stopping to point out the crag where the watchman had lit a fire to warn Clytemnestra that her lord had returned from Troy. Larks trilled overhead and sheep-bells tinkled in the crystal air. Then Aristotle led us through the Lion Gates and we were in the citadel itself.

I do not know just what I had expected, but my first reaction was one of disappointment; there was so little to see. Nothing in the way of splendour, only ruined walls, the dim outlines of an ancient fortress and some piles of stone. Nothing to suggest the stupendous events of two thousand years ago. But the moment of enchantment was to come. Aristolte pointed to the ground and there I saw two grooves worn by the passing of ancient chariot wheels. Agamemnon and his generals had passed that way when they had gone to Troy and it was from the crumbling battlements above our heads that Clytemnestra and her paramour had watched them go.

The centuries had vanished and the *Iliad* had come alive for me as it had done for Heinrich Schliemann when he opened the narrow burial shafts and lifted the golden mask that covered the face of Agamemnon. Doubts have since been cast on the accuracy of the little German archaeologist's claims, but nothing can deprive him of that moment, and I, for one, refuse to join the sceptics.

My own big moment came when Aristotle led us to an upper level in the citadel and pointed out a little chamber in the palace, dimly traced in stone. It was here, he said, that Clytemnestra had plunged the dagger into Agamemnon's throat as he lay in his bath. On that particular morning the grass, still glistening with dew, was thick with crimson anemones, for all the world like clots of blood and, for a moment, time dissolved and I was present at that stupendous moment twenty centuries ago.

Those flowers made a more lasting impression on me than the beehive tombs, despite their miraculous masonry and engineering skill, in the same way that the grooves in the paving near the Lion Gates spoke more eloquently of the past than even the gates themselves, which, in my opinion, scarcely seemed to warrant their impressive name.

Aristotle set the final seal upon the morning by showing us a disused cistern in the palace courtyard where he had hidden two Australian soldiers during the retreat of 1941, telling us very simply how he had brought them food and water and kept them alive. Almost without emotion, he told us how his ribs had been kicked in by a Nazi boot when he refused to reveal their hiding place, that his wife had been beaten and his children threatened, but no-one had been guilty of betrayal.

'Their names were Syd and Fred,' he said. 'I often wonder what became of them. They promised to write when they got home, but I never heard from them.'

Syd and Fred, I thought, if you are still alive is it possible that you forgot your promise to write to a little man called Aristotle who wonders why he has not heard from you? Knowing human nature, and especially my fellow-countrymen, I concluded that it very possibly was so.

After Mycenae came Tiryns. Here Hercules was born, and the massive walls are said to have been built by giants. It seemed difficult to credit that mere men could have piled those huge blocks of stone, without supernatural aid; but Tiryns was drab and uninspiring after Mycenae and a biting wind made us huddle in the lee of one of the walls. Then, apparently from nowhere,

141

a party of young men garlanded with flowers came along the road, singing and dancing, on their way to a wedding or a festival of their own. Seeing Gilda, they danced round her so that her face grew pink and she did not know which way to look. Observing her embarrassment, they good-naturedly dispersed and went on their way, shouting and dancing as they disappeared.

Then came Nauplion, with its ring of mountains casting their reflection in the blue of its bay, its minute island fortress shining in the sun. There was another, larger fortress on the summit of a rocky peak high above the town and four hundred steps to climb, narrow and steep, hewn out of the rockface. We found that a family was living up there, with children, hens, and of all unlikely things, a cow. How they managed to get it up those steps, unless it had then been a calf, was a mystery, and what good is a cow without a bull from time to time? There was no bull in sight when we were there, and artificial insemination was only in the experimental stage, so they either had to bring the gentleman up to her, or coax her down to him. Did they garland her with flowers like the young men at Tiryns?

Peering over the parapet, we could see the ghostly shape of ships still lying on the seabed, clearly visible though lying fathoms deep. They were relics of the great retreat of 1942 as Nauplion was one of the last ports held open for what remained of the defeated Allied army to escape. Far below us, singing as they went, a company of Greek soldiers went marching along the street, their strong young voices rising in the crisp spring air like an affirmation of survival.

It was a wonderful time, and Greece had cast her spell over me so that, afterwards, the suave elegance of Italy seemed slightly overblown, and the Colosseum vulgar in its opulence.

CHAPTER 16

We were met on the wharf at Tilbury by Eila and her son, two Australians who had preceded us to London by several weeks. Eila, good soul, had found a place for us to stay in, which was cheap and otherwise suitable but was away out in North Hendon; the bus took a good forty minutes to reach Piccadilly Circus which, to me, is London's heart. The landlady was severe, and I earned her disfavour by boiling an egg in the saucepan that was reserved for boiling milk! Quite clearly, we were not compatible and it was advisable to find somewhere less demanding.

Whether beneficent Jupiter had anything to do with it or not I do not know, but one day I felt an impulse to scramble down the stairs from the top of a London bus when it paused at the traffic lights at a place with the unlikely name of Swiss Cottage. I had noticed it in passing and had thought what fun it would be to have an address like that. Dodging the traffic, I walked boldly into an estate agent's office and asked if they had any flats to let.

Remember, this was early 1952. London was still in a ruinous state—rows of terraces were nothing but skeleton shells, whole streets were reduced to piles of rubble—so the housing shortage was acute and to ask for an empty flat was equivalent to asking for the Koh-i-Noor. The woman behind the desk looked slightly stunned, then took a closer look at me and seemed to recover her poise.

'You're in luck,' she said. 'Not half an hour ago someone came in and said they had a flat they wanted to let. There's a waiting list yards long, but I haven't had time to enter it in the book so I might as well give it to you. It's partly furnished, you know, and the rent is twenty-seven and six a week.'

'That'll do,' I said. 'Where is it?'

'In Fellows Road. It's only five minutes walk from here. I'll give you the address and you can go and have a look at it.'

The door was opened by an elderly woman with a Northern Irish face; I knew that because she had a strong resemblance to my grandfather Blayney, who had come from County Tyrone. She surveyed me rather severely from her deep-set eyes, then told me to come in. She led me into her sitting-room and told me to sit down while she questioned me about myself, who I was, and why I had come to London. I took in some details of the room. It was the very essence of an English drawing-room, with mahogany furniture, glass-fronted cabinets with china and Waterford crystal, a bow-shaped window through which I caught a glimpse of herbaceous borders and some fruit trees enclosed by a high brick wall.

Having been satisfied about my bona fides, she led me upstairs to inspect the vacant flat. It was a replica of her own, except that it lacked the elegant furniture and the fire burning cosily in the grate, but it had the same bow window looking down on the walled garden, and in the main bedroom there was an enormous wardrobe, a double bed without a mattress and a washstand with a marble top. There was a smaller bedroom, next to it a prehistoric bathroom, and a kitchen minus a gas stove. For twenty-seven and six a week it was a bargain, and Gilda and I moved in the following week.

Swiss Cottage is on the fringe of Hampstead Heath and its neighbours are Chalk Farm and Camden Town, not the rural retreats they had formerly been but a source of unending delight to me. High Street was lined with shops that sold secondhand furniture and there was a market at Camden Town where I met my first costers and experienced their caustic wit.

'What are you looking for, lady—diamonds?' one of them asked as I bent down to examine a bag of beans.

The secondhand furniture shops were full of antiques and I bought a walnut table beautifully inlaid with ivory, a *chaise-*

144

longue upholstered in faded brocade, a crinoline chair and a cabinet of bird's-eye maple for something like two hundred pounds.

I wished that I could buy everything in sight, ship it out to Australia and solve my financial problems for the next ten years. But there was no such easy solution: I had slightly more than three thousand pounds, the income from Aunt Belle's estate, and my talent as a writer. Not much with which to face the formidable task of finding work in London.

Gilda had to be sent to school. With the help of Florence James, a friend from my Sydney days, she was enrolled at a school in Golders Green known as the King Alfred, which was co-educational and run on modern lines inasmuch as the headmaster and mistress were called by their first names and a council was held each morning under an ancient oak where the pupils sat on logs and said what they felt about the shortcomings of their teachers and how they thought the curriculum could be improved. In spite of which some very exceptional young women and youths emerged, and Gilda appears to have suffered no harm.

It was said that it took two years and a lot of grit to find a niche in London; it took me the greater part of three. Meanwhile, I earned what I could by selling baby clothes and underwear in Selfridges. It was not difficult to get temporary employment there, especially during their periodic sales, and many Australians were glad to tide themselves over a crisis by such means. There was also a period in a china shop in Baker Street, not a happy time for me, as the 'lady' manageress took a dislike to me and took pleasure in sending me up a ladder to dust the top shelves. This, because of my fear of heights, brought on an attack of giddiness and a sweat of fear in case I sent one of the Doulton jugs or a Wedgwood plate crashing to the floor. Then I met someone who had an agency for American paperbacks of an extremely dubious kind, who paid me fifty pounds a time for transposing American porn into an appropriate English porn. It was the lowest form of literary activity and my gorge rose every time I committed the crime against my principles, but the constant drain on my resources had induced a state of panic, and principles had to go. When I was offered the job of publicity officer at the Embassy Theatre in Swiss Cottage, I felt that I could again lift up my head.

The Embassy Theatre at Swiss Cottage was, and still is, one of London's best known fringe theatres, where untried plays, many of which went on to the West End and international fame, first saw the footlights, and I nourished a secret hope that *The Touch of Silk* might one day join their ranks. But that was not to be. A succession of flops brought great discouragement to the entrepreneur who had hired the theatre for twelve months, and in spite of my efforts to lure an audience through its doors the footlights were dimmed, the doors of the Embassy closed, and I was once more out of work.

But in the meantime I had made two friends who were to remain staunch to me for the remainder of my life. Peggy and Teddy Cleven had managed the theatre club and were as bright and refreshing a pair as one could ever wish to meet. Peg was a perky little redhead from a farming family in Shropshire, while Teddy—six feet two in height—was a Belgian, born in Brussels. They were not long married, had a chubby baby boy called Andrew, and were besottedly in love with each other. Consequently everybody fell in love with them, especially myself. When the Embassy went dark, the Clevens had no problems finding another job, as a regular patron of the club had noted their efficiency as well as their charm and invited them to come and manage a cosy little pub he owned in Kent. So off they went to Birchington while I remained in Fellows Road and wondered where I was going to find another source of income.

I had given up all hope of finding work with the BBC, as the scripts I had submitted shortly after arriving in London had been firmly rejected on the score of being unsuitable for radio. This surprised me very much, as they had all been broadcast by the ABC and, in my opinion, the standard of radio drama in Australia compared very favourably with any I had heard emanating from Broadcast House. But the letter was signed by the Director of Drama, Val Gielgud, brother of the famous John, and against that there could be no argument. So I sought the help of a fellow Australian I had met in Australia House.

Allan Stranks was one of a number of expatriates who had come to London immediately after the war, and was then earning a substantial income by writing the story and dialogue for cartoon strips, as I had done for the *Sydney Morning Herald*, with this important difference: Allan was writing for the *Daily Express, The Mirror* and a number of other papers which sold millions of copies every day and was paid accordingly; he was also in no danger of being dispensed with as everything he wrote was syndicated and sold overseas.

He was a tall, easy-going Australian who complained of overwork and his inability to find a writer who would 'ghost' for him and give him some time to play a round of golf. I took note of this and knocked on his door one Sunday morning, hoping that he was not out playing golf. He was still in pyjamas and dressing-gown and was in need of a shave. He had clearly been working late, so was in a receptive frame of mind when I told him I was prepared to ghost for him and handed him a scrapbook in which I had pasted some cuttings from *The Conways*. He read some pages, then put the book aside.

'The reason why I can never find a ghost writer is that if they are good enough to ghost for me, they should be working for themselves', he said, and I felt my hopes begin to fade. But they rose when he added, 'I happen to know that the editor-in-chief of *Girl* is looking for someone to write for him. If you like, I'll give him a call and make a time for you to see him.'

Girl, as I already knew, was one of four phenomenally successful juvenile papers published in Great Britain. It consisted largely of highly coloured story-strips, was reputed to pay the highest space rates in Fleet Street and was almost impossible to break into. Now Allan Stranks was offering me an introduction to its chief editor, someone I had never hoped to meet. He made the appointment right away, and a few days later I was on my way down Fleet Street to the sweetest job I ever had in all my varied career.

Marcus Morris was one of the most colourful characters in Fleet Street. An ordained priest of the Church of England, *bon vivant*, professional ballroom dancer, aesthete, dandy, and connoisseur of women, he conformed to none of the conventions, and his publications, *Eagle, Girl, Swift* and *Robin*, had totally changed the previously held conception that children's comics should be crude, vulgar and frequently unpleasant. Appalled at the abysmal depths to which they had descended, he approached Edward Hulton, of the then thriving Hulton Press and showed him a dummy copy of the kind of comic he would publish instead— a less sensational but equally exciting illustrated weekly aimed at ten to fourteen-year-old boys. Edward Hulton liked the idea and gave him the go-ahead to put his theories into practice for a year. He did, and with such an outstanding success that *Eagle* was followed by one of its companion comics every year with a circulation that was the envy of all their competitors and made Marcus Morris something of a legend.

Although I wrote for him for something like five years, beyond that first brisk interview I rarely saw the great man; he remained aloof in his palatial suite and I dealt exclusively with the editress of *Girl*, Jean Crouch. It was said that Marcus chose his staff with regard to the shape of their legs, which may or may not be true, but I do know that all the female members that I saw were invariably young, good-looking and svelte, and Jean was no exception.

She was married to a man who practised as a psychiatrist. He was interested in lysergic acid and used his wife as the subject for his experiments. There was a certain demonic glare in his eyes and I had a feeling that had he lived in the Middle Ages he would have practised vivisection, and enjoyed it. I never grew fond of James, but was very fond of Jean and sometimes saw her on the morning following one of his investigations into the effects of the newly discovered drug, the end results of which had not yet been fully realised, but the dazed expression on her face and size of the pupils in her eyes should have warned him of the dangers ahead.

They lived in one of the elegant Nash terraces in Regent's Park and sublimated their desire for children by housing a swarm of Siamese cats and their numerous progeny. The smell of cats' pee, stale cat food, and a suggestion of fresh shit greeted the caller whenever they opened the door. The original pair were called Oedipus and Jocasta, with good reason; they were allowed to breed with no regard to age or consanguinity, and the expensive furniture, originally bought from Heales, had its upholstery ripped to shreds by feline claws, then was liberally sprayed with feline piss.

At one stage, Jean conceived a passion for a hamster, which was allowed to wander at will around the flat. One of James's patients trod on it and broke its leg, and as Jean was late for an appointment and unable to take it to the vet, she put it in her make-up box, called a taxi, and off it went on the back seat to have the damage repaired. After that, it was kept in the bath, and if anyone wanted to bathe, the poor little creature had to be caught and shut up in a biscuit tin until ablutions were complete. Finally it died, rather to everyone's relief, including Jean's.

The celebrated terraces in Regent's Park are part of the Royal Estate, and while there are no restrictions on the number of cats the tenants may choose to keep, Jean and James had to seek royal assent before they could repaint the kitchen cupboards and put up an extra shelf. What would Queen Elizabeth have thought had she seen the carnage at number 73? But one should remember the royal corgies, who are reputed to be badly house-trained.

Somehow Jean managed to edit *Girl*, until James left to pursue his experiments in Chicago. Very wisely, Jean decided to go with him, and *Girl* passed into other hands. I don't know how Jean ended up, but she looked very strange when I saw her last.

Not long after moving into Fellows Road, I met George Nicholson. Norman Haire was indirectly responsible for this.

I had written to Norman soon after I arrived in London and he invited me to visit him in Harley Street, warning me to expect a change in him since he had lived in Ithaca Road. He had suffered a severe coronary the year before and was on a diet that had reduced him to a ghost of himself. Nevertheless, it was a shock to see the formerly portly man looking pale and haggard, with his clothes hanging loosely on his frame and his collar several sizes too large for his neck. But his zeal for advocating liberated sex was unabated, and he invited me to come and hear a lecture he was giving in Red Lion Square. Knowing that a lecture by Norman Haire was bound to attract a crowd, I made a point of being there in good time. The foyer was crowded by the time that I arrived, as the hall was a popular venue, where all manner of cults and cranks proselytised their views, and Norman was not the only one to give a lecture that night. Unsure of where to go, I asked a man standing by himself if he could tell me where Dr Norman Haire would speak. He looked surprised at being addressed by a strange woman, but recovered enough to tell me that it was on the upper floor and that he was going there himself.

As we went up the stairs together he told me that he was a former patient of Norman's and I wondered if he had a sexual problem of some sort. He looked normal enough, not bad-looking, well-dressed, with every appearance of affluence, typical English upper middle class—thus I summed him up as he talked. I told him I had recently arrived from Australia and was staying in Hendon North. Norman delivered his lecture, which was much the same as the one I had heard in Sydney and, to my surprise, the Englishman was waiting at the foot of the stairs as I came down. He asked could he drive me home.

Norman had invited me to come to his house for supper, which was a signal mark of approval, and I had either to risk offending him or say 'no, thank you' to my new acquaintance.

The choice was obvious. I did not invite him to come in but gave him my telephone number, feeling a sense of excitement. He was so much the kind of man I had hoped to meet, though the thought had been far from my mind when I had spoken to him. It was sheer chance that I did.

He telephoned a few days later and took me out to dinner in a pleasant little place in Soho, and I learned who and what he was. He was a fully ordained minister of the Church of England! He was eager to talk, as though he wanted to avoid any future misunderstandings, and I learnt that he was married but was separated from his wife, had two children whom he never saw but missed very much. The marriage had foundered not because of any misdemeanour on his part. He was the heir to a large fortune and was managing his father's spinning mills in Lancashire when he married, and all had gone well until he received a 'call' to serve the Lord. It had happened quite suddenly, while he was travelling in a train. So he quit the firm and entered a college of theology in order to dedicate himself to God.

His father was furious and changed his will, and his wife, quite naturally, showed no enthusiasm for life in a country vicarage instead of the comfortable mansion she was accustomed to and refused to have anything more to do with him. So he had formed a relationship with another woman which had lasted for several years. Now she had unaccountably grown tired of him and brought it to an end. This had distressed him very much and, having failed to find a substitute for her, he had sought advice from Norman Haire. Norman had told him to go to a good tailor, buy himself a more impressive car than his rather run-down Austin—he now drove a Rover—and come to the lecture in Red Lion Square. Then I had come up and spoken to him and it seemed like the hand of Fate. I think he said 'pre-ordained'.

It is difficult to account for my reaction to these astonishing revelations, but with every word that tumbled from his mouth, my opinion of him changed until I began to feel actual distaste. Why did I respond in such a way when I had remained unmoved by any of the excesses of Kings Cross? Here was an honest man, a decent man, whose only crime was failure to observe the seventh commandment, and what did I, a proclaimed agnostic, care about the seventh or any of the other nine?

Did I feel outraged because he was a man of God, the same as Roberta's lover had been, or because he was not the successful businessman I had taken him to be? If he had worn his collar in reverse, would I have selected him out of the crowd in Red Lion Square? Whatever the answer is, I never forgave him and never allowed him the slightest liberty, not even a casual peck on the cheek.

He did not give up easily. In fact he was extremely nice to me. He fixed the flue in the gas heater in the bathroom, which was nothing less than lethal, built a shelf for my books, and complained that I never gave him a chance to 'be nice' to me. Hopefully, he took Gilda and me to spend a weekend in his vicarage in Berkshire. We slept in an attic room that had clearly been the love nest, prepared with much care and thought for the former mistress. There was a rosy lampshade above the bed that cast a becoming glow over the occupant, the pillows were filled with down, and the mattress was as yielding and voluptuous as the one I had left behind in the house at Castlecrag, but the thought of sharing it with the man who slept in the adjoining room was totally unacceptable and Gilda and I slept soundly there instead.

Of course, he finally got tired of this unrewarding situation and ceased to come to Fellows Road. I met him accidentally a few months afterwards. He was looking well and told me that two of his parishioners, a widow and her daughter aged sixteen, were now living in the vicarage and that they all knelt in prayer each night before they went to bed.

Winter came and we too had a fire smouldering cosily in the grate, but, like most pleasant things in life, this had its price, in my case, labouring up two flights of stairs each day with a bucket of coal in either hand, to say nothing of clearing the grate of its residue of coke and raising a cloud of dust that settled on the carpet and furniture and choked the lungs. The weather had been reasonably mild until after the New Year, then winter closed its iron jaws. The Serpentine froze over and the streets were slippery with ice; in addition, there was the February fog.

What we call fog in Australia is no more than a pleasant mountain mist compared to a 'London particular', and the one that swaddled London in 1953 was a classic of its kind. It had gathered momentum for several days and reached its peak in mid-afternoon. Street lamps became a faint glow that shed no light, traffic ground to a halt and the Underground became the sole means of transport. I got out at Belsize Park and emerged to face a solid wall of evil yellow murk. Visibility was almost nil, and I had to find my way to Fellows Road, which was something like half a mile away.

It was a daunting prospect and while I was standing irresolute, a bus crept cautiously into sight. It was preceded by the ticket-collector, who carried a flaring torch he had contrived from a rolled-up newspaper. A pile of *Evening Standards* had been abandoned at the entrance to the Underground. He paused to collect a fresh supply and, without a word, continued to pilot the bus as it crept blindly towards its haven at the depot. It was an eerie sight, and I braced myself to face the ordeal of reaching home. Fellows Road, I knew, was on my right, but landmarks there were none. I had to rely on instinct and a sense of touch as I groped my way along the street, my fingers brushing against the iron railing outside invisible houses.

All went well until I had to cross a street, and having advanced a step or two I was seized by a sudden sense of panic. Deprived of the railing, all sense of direction deserted me, I did not know which way to go—I was totally disoriented. The opposite curb was obliterated, and there was no way of telling in which direction it lay and nothing to do but shuffle my way ahead and I was rewarded by feeling the toe of my shoe strike something solid. It was the curb, and not far off was the iron railing to guide me to Fellows Road. I finally found number 52, and thankfully stumbled up the steps and in the door. I had been worried about Gilda, but the King Alfred School had had the sense to abandon classes at midday and she was seated before the fire making toast when I got in.

It was one of the last of the traditional 'pea-soupers', as a by-law was subsequently passed prohibiting the use of coal fires that belched their fumes from millions of chimneypots all over

London. But it did not come soon enough to save the fat cattle that were exhibited that year in the annual Earl's Court show. Despite the efforts of their frantic owners, which included the use of oxygen and gas masks, the poor beasts choked to death in the lethal fog.

Even an English winter comes to an end eventually, and when August arrived, and with it Gilda's summer vacation, it was time to pack a bag and set off to the Continent, starting, of course, with Paris, of which I had barely caught a glimpse when Guido and I were on our way back from Moscow in 1934.

We had been given the address of a modest hotel where Oscar Wilde was said to have spent the final years of his exile. It was rather run-down now, and probably had been when its distinguished guest had occupied one of its upstairs rooms, but it was within a stone's throw of Notre Dame, whose majestic buttresses and Gothic towers cast their shadow over a narrow-fronted shop which had *Shakespeare Press* written above its door and gave me tremors of delight. But August is not a good month to be in Paris—it is very hot and all the galleries and little restaurants one has been told to patronise are closed. All Paris, it seems, has departed for *l'annuel*, choking the roads with traffic and being a source of great frustration to the tourist as yet unversed in the customs of the French.

The logical thing to do was go somewhere else, which we did, stopping off at Chartres en route to the chateaux of the Loire. Money was short, so we travelled by bus and stayed at youth hostels along the way. The first of these was at Tours. The bus stopped in the centre of the town and with a valise slung between us on a length of stick, we walked between an avenue of chestnuts to the stately Chateau Graumont, once the country retreat of a nobleman but now reduced to the status of a youth hostel. Turreted and towered, surrounded by acres of parkland, it must surely be unique, and we spent several nights there for the equivalent in francs of a few shillings a night. We slept on narrow stretchers in what had once been the ballroom, and cooked our breakfast on a gas ring in the ancient kitchens.

It was a lot of fun, though there was very little sleep as a youth orchestra was billeted there and rehearsed for hours each night, and fresh arrivals, the forerunners of the present backpackers, kept arriving from all quarters of the globe, switching on the lights above our heads and showing no interest in going to bed.

But we slept in luxury one night. It was in a tiny village called Azay le Rideaux which was famous for its mediaeval chateau and formal gardens. Having decided to economise, we tried to hitch a ride there but met with no success. Cars and trucks whizzed past and took no notice of our thumbs—we even got a black look or two from righteous matrons sitting in the back seat. We gave up the attempt when a bus appeared, and we carefully enquired the time it would return to Tours. 'Neuf heures' the driver said but forgot to say 'a demain'. So we stood in the street at Azay le Rideaux and watched the hands of the clock in the tower go past the hour and on and on, and no bus came.

There was what looked like a tavern further down the street. We peered through the open door and down an unlit passage to a room where the sound of loud male voices scared us off. The only alternative was a small but picturesque hotel, from which emanated an air of luxury and expense. We had no luggage and very little money, but I had some traveller's cheques. We would undoubtedly be looked on as suspicious characters by the canny French *hotelier*, arriving as we did so late at night, on foot and unaccompanied by a man. The alternatives were either sleeping in the park or risking the noisy tavern down the road, so hand-in-hand we ventured in. Sure enough, the *patron* eyed us dubiously, then went to get his wife. She was a motherly soul who spoke a little English and accepted our explanation. Yes, traveller's cheques were accepted, and did we require some dinner? A meal in such a place would ruin our budget, I thought, but we were ravenous, so why not?

It was a meal to dream about, and the room that we were shown into afterwards was an elegant version of rural France. We sat on the edge of the bed and rocked with laughter. We had tried to hitch in order to save a bus fare and ended up spending a small fortune on a bed and a meal. But Jupiter came to my aid. The motherly woman had a daughter the same age as Gilda who was being sent to England to complete her education. Would I, *could* I possibly shepherd her to London, where she would be met by her aunt? Of course I could, and after that any mention of traveller's cheques was waved aside. We had breakfast of coffee and bread rolls and arranged for the girl to meet us in Tours in a few days' time. But the rendezvous did not take place, as a sudden strike paralysed all transport throughout the whole of France, and Gilda and I had a nightmare journey back home.

The lure of Europe was irresistible, and we went to Italy, Spain, and even as far as Yugoslavia, sleeping upright in third-class carriages, staying in third-class pensiones or hotels, eating in dubious restaurants, but forgetting the discomforts at the sight of the Pitti Palace, St Mark's Square, the Alhambra, and the Vatican in Rome. I had waited fifty years to see them, and I saw them all.

CHAPTER 17

The 'long period of chastity' that now prevailed did not unduly trouble me as, with London at my door, I had plenty to divert me; also I was fifty years of age and, despite my youthful appearance, the inner fires had begun to cool. I still looked at an attractive man and wondered what he would be like in bed, but felt no urgent need to discover.

A further alleviating circumstance was Gilda. To the best of my knowledge, she still retained her innocence, but she was sixteen and that would undoubtedly change, possibly quite soon. My way of life, though rich in experience and colourful, was not the kind that I would choose for her. A good, sound marriage, a peaceful, uneventful life, though tedious at times, was preferable, in my mind, to the turmoil of mine. There was too much pain in it, too little happiness, and happiness to me was the measure of success, regardless of who you were or what you did.

I was now moderately happy, and felt I had achieved a moderate success. I was in London, the city of my dreams; I lived in a pleasant place, I had made a few congenial friends, I liked my work, and I even had two cats!

Chloe and Mandy were an enchanting pair of pedigree Persians I had bought in a reckless moment at a cat show soon after settling in at Fellows Road. It was love at first sight. Unable to choose between the two, I had bought them both and carried them home in a cardboard box, set them loose in the walled garden and watched them make good use of the herbaceous borders before transporting them inside, after which they settled in. Chloe slept on my feet each night while Mandy went to bed with Gilda. Chloe was a sybarite and preferred to bask on a cushion, while Mandy went off to discover what lay beyond the garden wall. While the Battle of Britain raged, the wall had been hit by a stray bomb, which left a gaping hole that was altogether too much for an inquisitive little cat, who scrambled over the rubble to make friends with her neighbours. One of them, a man in his early forties, brought her back.

There was a certain feline element in Howard Healy's make-up. He loved comfort and elegant living, had a slightly malicious streak and a lot of charm, and took an unfailing interest in other people's lives. This he displayed by asking me innumerable questions about myself and what I was. Unlike the majority of English people, he had no prejudice against Australians; he had a cousin who had married one of them and lived in Sydney and appeared to have survived. For my part, I found him charming. He was one of those blue-eyed, fair-haired Englishmen whose age is difficult to judge, not particularly good-looking but pleasantly tanned as a result of having spent the summer on the Côte d'Azur. I was particularly struck by his ready smile and beautiful white teeth.

Everything was fine about him, with one exception: he was clearly and unmistakeably a homosexual.

Homosexuals had figured very little in my life before that time. That they existed in Australia was undeniable, but almost without exception they were found in the *corps de ballet* or the chorus line. Any who existed beyond that restricted field were inconspicuous and few people became aware of them. They were the butt of snide jokes and feeble wit. 'Did you hear about poor Walter's accident? He fell down in Collins Street and got up himself!' was typical of them.

They were considered freaks and of little consequence, but now here was one of them, and he was intelligent, sophisticated, witty—just the kind of man I liked. I might have felt otherwise had I not reached the age where sex is no longer of prime importance. And I felt only relief that I would not be called upon to go to bed with him and go through the old routine of wearing seductive underwear, shaving my legs and changing the sheets next day.

Soon after Mandy's introduction I met his partner, Bob. Bob

was a gentle, dreamy sort of being who had a gift for making curtains and re-covering chairs, which was very useful as he and Howard had bought a number of houses that had been partly ruined by the air raids and were restoring them with a view to letting them as furnished rooms and cleaning up a fortune. The house next door was one of them, but Howard was not living there when Mandy wandered in; he had merely been seeing how the restoration was progressing. Bob took no exception to me and I took no exception to him—indeed I rarely saw him.

But Howard became an important factor in my life. He had a small but exquisite Georgian house not far from where Keats had lived and heard the nightingales on Hampstead Heath. Howard had no nightingales, but he had an aviary filled with tiny twittering birds in the garden behind his house, Coalport and Meissen china in his rosewood cabinets, and a four-poster bed with velvet hangings in his bedroom—I glimpsed it through the open door, but never went inside. He was witty and made jokes about himself in a slightly bawdy way, could charm a waiter into finding us a table when the restaurant was full, also seemed to get good seats without ever having to join a queue. He was a sophisticate above all other things, and I was flattered, because he seemed to like being seen with me. He was also good for Gilda, and treated her as though she was a favourite niece, teased her, scolded her if she neglected her appearance, took an interest in her work at school and agreed with my idea of what her future should be.

'Get her married,' was his verdict when she was going out on her first date and looked particularly good.

There is a short street immediately behind the underground in Leicester Square whose name I cannot remember. The Theatre Arts Club was situated there and I became a member as soon as I could afford the fee. It was not a great amount and provided privileges far in excess of what one would expect. It had a small but adequate theatre where some of the newest plays, as yet untested in the West End, got a trial run, a restaurant where meals were good and reasonably priced, and a clubroom where members could drink to a late hour or sit and read the *Spotlight* or the *Daily Telegraph*. I loved the Theatre Arts and took Howard there on a number of occasions, generally after a matinée or a concert at the Festival Hall.

On one particular afternoon we had been to see *Around the World in Eighty Days*. It was an amusing film, and left us in a happy mood. The clubroom was crowded, but we were able to find a window-seat unoccupied, which was a stroke of luck. The late afternoon sun shone through the window and fell on his face and I thought how attractive he looked and admired his beautiful teeth. At seven o'clock we parted, I to go to a meeting at Australia House, Howard to visit a friend—he did not say who. After the meeting, I went home and slept soundly until the telephone rang next morning. Bob's voice was at the other end.

'Betty, I have dreadful news for you. Howard is dead,' he said.

No-one will ever know what he did or said to the two plain-clothes detectives lurking in the men's lavatory in the Leicester Square underground, but I can picture the scene quite well. They would make some flippant remark to him and he would respond in kind. I knew his love of a bawdy joke so well. Perhaps he accompanied it with an obscene gesture, perhaps he did make an overture to them. Whatever the provocation, he was taken away in a paddy-wagon and charged with offensive behaviour committed in a public place.

Bob was not at home, but Howard's solicitor came and bailed him out, after which he drove him back to his house and left him at the door. I can never bear to think of the state of mind that he was in, or the hell he went through before he went into the bathroom, cut the gas pipe with a pair of pliers, lay down with a blanket over his head, and died.

Guido and Ethel were in London at the time. I had not seen them but knew where they were, and after the cremation I went to them for help. I don't know how I looked, but they barely recognised the black-clad woman standing at the door. It was a bleak London day. I sat before the fire and tried to explain what had happened. They thought that I had lost a lover, but I had lost more than that: I had lost all hope that life was going to relent and give me back my happiness.

I was bitter and resentful. I had lowered my standards and been prepared to compromise. Howard fell far short of the kind of man I had hoped for but I had been willing to accept him for what he was and not ask for more. 'Am I not to be allowed even *that*?' I asked. I grew morbid and wondered if I was the accursed of Aphrodite and had offended her in a former life, perhaps I had been a man who had done some woman or women a great injury, so that Aphrodite had condemned me to live again as a woman and learn what it was like to suffer at the hands of men?

Childish and illogical, perhaps, but I was deeply shocked and in an abnormal state of mind. Luckily I had enough sound common-sense to realise what it was and that it must be stopped. The surest way of doing this was to get away from Fellows Road and start a fresh life somewhere else. I did not go very far. There was a fine old mansion at the top of Fitzjohn's Avenue, not five minutes' walk from Hampstead Heath. It stood in a beautiful garden and had known better days, as it had been converted into a number of one-roomed flats. I took a large one on the ground floor for myself and a smaller one upstairs for Gilda. The treatment worked. I was asked to write the story for a page in *Swift*, another Marcus Morris brainchild, which left me less time to brood about the vengeance of Aphrodite. Sanity returned.

In some ways, I regretted leaving Fellows Road, as I had grown fond of the two old ladies who lived on the lower floor. One of them was Mrs Beecher, who had questioned me about my bona fides before she would let me see the flat, the other was her sister whom I only knew as 'Sis'. She was what could be called peculiar. She always wore the same fusty-coloured dress, an apron and a woollen cardigan, and what looked like a knitted tea-cosy on her head. It was difficult to tell her age because I never saw her hair and she had lost all of her teeth, but she was very agile and insisted on rushing to the door whenever anybody knocked and telling them that there was nobody at home before she slammed it in their face. This annoyed her sister very greatly, and she would seize her by the arm, shut her in her bedroom and make profound apologies to the astonished visitor.

Poor Sis, she was undoubtedly a virgin and became man-mad as time went on. Howard had had a profound effect on her; she got quite coy whenever she saw him and, once, she opened the door of her room as he went past, threw herself on the floor, her skirt thrown over her head, and called out: 'Man! Man!' Even Howard's customary aplomb deserted him; he hurried up the stairs and looked quite shaken at this manifestation of female desperation.

Mrs Beecher, slightly younger, was still alert and bright. Sis was a great trial to her, and she used to complain to me about the way she would steal into the kitchen and turn out the gas when a roast was cooking in the oven, or forget to turn off the tap in the bathroom and flood the floor. Sis would be sent around the corner to the grocer's shop armed with a basket and a list of things required. One day she got lost and was brought back to Fellows Road in a police car. This was a high moment in her life.

'I was brought home in a taxi by *two* gentlemen,' she said with a wicked gleam in her eye. After that, she was not allowed out alone.

Bit by bit, Mrs Beecher also told me about herself. She came from Northern Ireland, Belfast, I think it was, and belonged to the family that manufactured Old Bleach linen, a name I already knew, as Grandfather Blayney had always slept in Old Bleach linen sheets, a guarantee of quality. Bundles of linen sheets and frilled pillowcases arrived from time to time at Fellows Road, some of them slightly flawed, and Mrs Beecher would pass some on to me in an apologetic way, fearing I might take offence. At Irish linen sheets!

She had a niece called Mary, of whom she was very fond, and showed me a picture of her taken when she was a bride— a lovely girl in a smother of lace and billowing satin.

'I seldom see her now,' said Mrs Beecher sadly. 'You see, she married this man in Africa, Professor Leakey'.

I did not know that I was looking at the bride of Louis Seymour Leakey, one of the world's great anthropologists, or that Mary, Mrs Beecher's niece, also an anthropologist, was to find a skull on an island in Lake Victoria that upset all previous calculations of the age of homo sapiens by several million years.

Poor Mrs Beecher was a devout Christian and hoped that Gilda and I would go to church with her on Sundays, but she went alone, carrying her C. of E. prayerbook, a neat figure in her tailored suit, hatted and veiled and wearing low-heeled leather shoes.

Gradually, I learned the details of her married life. Her husband had been an engineer and had worked on the construction of some reservoirs in Wales. 'We were very happy,' she said simply. Then came 1914 and the war. 'Mick felt he ought to go, and I told him if he felt that way he should join up. He went to London and paid five hundred pounds to join the Sportsmen's Regiment. They did their training in the ballroom of the Savoy Hotel. It wasn't very long before they were sent to France. I got word to say that he was seriously wounded. They let me go to see him . . .' The old voice faltered there and her hands moved convulsively in her lap. 'He did not get better . . .'

She was distressed when I told her I was going, and gave me a copper-lustre jug and teapot to remember her by, and I felt bad about leaving her. But all ended happily. Her husband's nephew, John, moved into the flat when I moved out. He was a grave young man, who would go to church with her and speak sternly to Sis whenever she misbehaved.

CHAPTER 18

I can think of no more desirable place in which to live than Hampstead, so after the initial shock of Howard's death had passed, life in Fitzjohn's Avenue was pleasant enough. It was difficult to feel depressed when walking over the Heath, and the winding streets and Tudor cottages were an unending delight. The extra work for *Swift* was another form of therapy, as it left me less time to grieve, and it also doubled my income so that I could afford to buy a car. Nothing spectacular, just an outdated Vauxhall sedan picked at random from a dealer's yard. But the Roland luck held good, it was sound in valve and cylinder, and it served me faithfully until I was seduced by the sight of a spanking new late-model Hillman Minx, seen in a showroom window in Piccadilly. But that was years ahead. 'Gentle Annie', as she was called, rolled uncomplainingly over the hills and dales of England, Wales and Scotland and I eventually sold her for fifty pounds to the man who came to fix the television set, and I trust he treated her well.

My affluence was further increased when I was asked to write another cartoon strip, this time for the *Daily Express*, which made me feel that I rivalled Allan Stranks, and I walked along Fleet Street like a conqueror. At fifty-four years of age, I, Betty Roland, an unknown from Australia, without influence or favour, had won her spurs in that Street of Ink where others, better equipped with better credentials, and above all usually male, had failed. My self-esteem was at an all-time high.

The committee meeting I had attended after saying goodbye to Howard outside the Theatre Arts Club was chaired by Ian Bevan, one of the many young Australians who lost no time in hurrying off to London at the end of the recent war. He had been on the staff of the *Sydney Morning Herald* and no doubt had his sights set on Fleet Street, instead of which he became one of London's leading theatrical agents, with clients of the calibre of Tommy Steele and 'the girl from Tiger Bay'. These triumphs were still to come; meanwhile, he had helped to found the Society of Australian Authors, which met every month at Australia House and had the blessing of the Agent-General, Sir Thomas White, himself an author, who allowed us to meet in the library until it was discovered that some of the books were missing and we were asked to transfer ourselves to the big hall on the ground floor.

The library had a pleasant, friendly atmosphere that may have accounted for the numbers who attended the monthly lectures and discussions, and were given a cup of tea and a piece of cake. No admission was charged. And, while the numbers did not diminish when we met in the big auditorium downstairs, nothing was quite the same, except the tea and cake.

One night, a distinguished-looking man came and spoke to me while I was pouring out the tea. He said his name was Kester Berwick.

'I have been wanting to meet you ever since I saw you take a bow in the Australia Theatre in Adelaide,' he said.

Immediately, I was transported back to May 1930, when I was still married to Ellis Davies. I had come to Adelaide to see the Repertory Theatre there put on a three-night season of *The Touch of Silk*. Overwhelmed by the applause when the curtain fell, I had been unable to say a word, but had stood there, surrounded by flowers, bowing, smiling stiffly, and blinking away my tears. Kester, too, remembered every detail, even the colour of the dress I wore: a soft shade of green with a green velvet jacket trimmed with white fox fur! He had also retained his high opinion of my play. That alone was enough to make me like him.

No-one in London, not even one of the Australians lined up for cups of tea, had even heard of *The Touch of Silk*, or if they had they made no mention of it. This no longer troubled me, but to meet someone who had seen it, liked it, and, twenty-four years afterwards, still remembered how its author looked astonished me, and I was deeply touched. Perhaps I was already half in love with him before the evening ended.

I was not the only woman in Australia House that night to be attracted by his charm and fine aesthetic face, but I was the one he seemed to favour, and I saw a lot of him in the following weeks. It was a slow maturing of a friendship, with no need of haste and a strong feeling of affinity. We were the same age, shared so many tastes, especially a love of theatre. He, too, had written plays and been disappointed, and while I had diverted myself with the Pangloss Theatre in Castlecrag, Kester had been involved with the Ab Intra Studio in Adelaide, a small experimental theatre that he had helped to found and had now shut down. We shared a love of all things Greek and talked about living on an island in the Aegean. Someday.

The feeling of inner peace that, for a brief time, I had had with Guido and Alan Williamson returned, and I began to think about a future life with him. No suggestion of this ever passed between us, nor did I give any sign of the increasing strength of the emotions he roused in me. He had beautiful hands and, one day, I watched him pick up Gilda's guitar and fondle it as a lover would fondle a woman, and felt my flesh respond as though he was caressing me. I wanted to take that hand and lay it on my breast, but did not do so.

I knew he lived in West Hampstead but had not given the matter much thought, but when he suggested that, for a change, I should come to visit him, I felt a sudden interest. What sort of life did he lead when he was not with me?

I was a little taken aback by the run-down appearance of the terrace house, the shabby carpet in the hall, and the fusty-looking paper on the wall. He lived on the second floor and led me up the stairs, apologising for the state of the linoleum and dingy light. He opened a door and stood aside to let me in.

I saw a scantily furnished room with a gas stove in one corner and a kitchen sink and an inner room that was a bedroom. It had a line of washing hanging up to dry and a double bed that had recently been slept in, and standing at the foot was a youth with tousled hair and rumpled clothes as though he has just woken up. It was John Tasker.

'Hello John,' said Kester in surprise. 'I didn't know that you were here.'

'I wasn't feeling well,' said John.

Kester lit the gas and put the kettle on to boil and we all had tea, with wholewheat biscuits. I suppose we talked quite amicably about different things. John probably told me that he was a student at the London School of Speech and Drama, that he did not particularly want to be an actor but hoped to be a director when he went back to Australia, which he did and met with considerable successes, the first of which was directing the original performance of Patrick White's *Ham Funeral.* Kester drank his tea and smiled benignly on us both, adding the information that John had been his pupil when he had taught drama at the Newcastle School of Arts. They had spent a year in Austria together, in a tiny village not far from Innsbruck, and he showed me some photos of them both, wearing *liederhosen* and Tyrolean hats.

I have no clear recollection of what was actually said, as I was numb with shock, but the basic facts are true, as I learned later on.

Kester did indeed teach John the rudiments of acting while they were in Newcastle and how to overcome an impediment in his speech. He also took him to the Tyrol, where he learnt a little German and met two old gentlewomen living in a little *schloss* with a red tower. They belonged to the von Minkus family, which had been ruined by the Treaty of Versailles so that all that remained of their former estates was the *schloss* with the red tower, formerly a hunting lodge. It was John's first experience of elegance and made a lasting impression on him.

After some idyllic weeks in the Tyrol, he and Kester came to London, where John applied for a grant to pay for tuition at the London School of Speech and Drama and Kester received an appointment to teach drama at the City Literary Institute three nights a week. It was on one of his free nights that we had met in Australia House. His attitude to John was that of an indulgent parent rather than a lover, and I doubt that it was ever more than that, and though John sometimes behaved like a spoilt and fractious child, it was impossible not to like him, though I inwardly resented him and had fits of jealousy at times, which I was careful to conceal.

It never occurred to either of them that I should be anything other than mildly surprised at finding John in the dingy bedroom that first afternoon. He was utterly unselfconscious, held out his hand and said he was so pleased to meet me, as Kester had told him about *The Touch of Silk* and how much he admired it. And I smiled and muttered something in response while Kester beamed proudly on us both.

And so began a three-way friendship that lasted for many years but was more spontaneous on their part than on mine.

There is something ludicrous about a woman in her middle fifties imagining a man was going to marry her because he had paid her a little attention and said a few flattering things, and I was thankful that I had given no indication of my unfounded hopes. But it was a warning that I was vulnerable, that I might be reaching the stage of desperation that would lead me to the extremes that poor little Sis had resorted to in Fellows Road. It was a sobering thought and I resolved to be on my guard in future and not indulge in foolish fantasies. With three deadlines to meet each week I had very little time to worry about the future and they also provided an excuse for curtailing our leisurely strolls on Hampstead Heath or visits to a gallery. Kester did not demur, he may even have been relieved, though we did meet from time to time, generally in Australia House, and John came with us to Kew Gardens on one occasion and we drank tea out of a thermos and ate the ubiquitous wheatmeal biscuits in the shade of a flowering cherry tree.

I cannot be sure how long it was after that when I realised I was earning a lot of money but had no time in which to enjoy it. Then Allan Stranks went for a holiday in Spain, played golf on a hot day and had a heart attack and died. I took this as a warning, so told the *Daily Express* that I did not wish to continue writing the daily strip for them and went for a holiday in Cochem, a picturesque town near the junction of the Rhine and the Moselle. It was autumn and the grapes had all been harvested so there was a wine festival almost every day in one of the little towns that cluster along the banks of those two legendary rivers. A memory remains of two riotous and inebriated weeks spent in cool darkened cellars, in taverns and village squares, dancing in circles round an effigy of Bacchus, coming home at midnight and hearing sounds of singing in the streets till dawn. But I had learnt caution. I could climb the stairs unaided, nobody came home with me, the kisses were restricted to a cheek and not responded to. Nevertheless, I was still vulnerable and when Adrian Forbes arrived at my door I did not send him away.

CHAPTER 19

Adrian was one of the interesting men that Alan Williamson
had introduced me to. J. Arthur Rank had sent him out from
England to make a documentary film about contemporary life
in the different cities in Australia and Alan described him as
something of a *rara avis* in that he not only directed his films
but also wrote the scripts, so we might possibly work together.
That did not happen, but the Castlecrag house was used as a
background for one of the sequences, which pleased me very
much.

Adrian also pleased me very much, but in an impersonal way.
I was quite content with Alan, and I knew that Adrian had some
woman sharing his flat in Elizabeth Bay—a cause of some disquiet
to Alan, who knew there was a wife at home in England and
that, should they be discovered, these extra marital relations would
be frowned upon by the right-thinking Mr Rank. And discovered
they were, in a most distressing way.

The film had been shot, the cameras packed away, and Adrian
was ready to fly back to England, so Alan gave a farewell dinner
at Romano's. All the crew were there, their assorted wives and
girlfriends and, of course, author-director Adrian Forbes. Half-
way through dinner he was called to the telephone and came
back looking like a man who had just received a sentence of
death. But the death was not his, it was that of the woman who
had shared his flat. He had evidently made it clear to her that
their relationship was at an end, and she had thrown herself under
a train at Central Station.

There had been an inquest and the whole miserable story
was splattered across the pages of the less reputable press, the
name of J. Arthur Rank being given great prominence. Not long
after that the disaster of Norman Rydge and Pagewood Studios

171

broke over my head, and Adrian Forbes and his fate were forgotten.

His unannounced arrival at my door was not altogether a surprise, however, as I had heard indirectly that he was working in a studio in Finchley, making shorts and two-minute spots for commercial television, a rather lowly occupation for a man who had travelled the world as a film VIP. His appearance prompted the thought that he must have found it hard to take. He didn't exactly have a hang-dog look, it was more apologetic, as though he felt that he should not be there but hoped I would not send him away.

He told me later that he had not telephoned because he knew that it was easier to snub a disembodied voice than a person in the flesh. Which, of course, is true but I doubt that I would have snubbed him, as I was genuinely glad to see him; he was a link with a happier past and I also wanted to know what had happened to him. The affair in Sydney was sad, and there could be no doubt that he had not behaved too well, but my sympathy had not been altogether with the woman who threw herself under the train. Women were always being dumped by men, and had to get over it; she must have been a bit neurotic; there was even a suggestion of that at the inquest. She had been in a psychiatric ward at one time, and it was Adrian's bad luck that he got involved with such a bad risk. Alan and I had agreed upon that point and felt a little sorry for him. Now, here he was, almost ten years later, standing at my door, hoping to be told to come inside.

He was not disappointed and we had finished what remained of a bottle of Gordon's gin before Gilda came in from school. She showed no surprise at finding a strange man sitting in a chair as though he had no intention of going home that night. But he did go home that night, and on the following occasions when he chose to call in as he passed, now feeling confident enough to telephone before he did.

I liked him. He was attractive and amusing and I could sense his desire for me, though he made no attempt to break through the invisible barrier I erected between us. He knew that his record

172

was bad and that I was wary of him, and he continued to sit on the opposite side of the hearth and observe me with watchful eyes. It grew more and more difficult to keep up my guard. I was sick of my unnatural chastity, and was still affected by the surge of sexuality that Kester Berwick had been responsible for and so unaccountably rebuffed.

It was quite late when Adrian arrived one night. Gilda had already gone to her room upstairs and I was about to go to bed. He had been making a film at an air force base somewhere and there had been an explosion. No-one had been killed but a piece of metal had struck him on the shin, which was bandaged and showed where the blood was seeping through. It was not much, but enough to lend some drama when he showed it to me. It had a strong effect on me. Why that should be so, I can't explain. Perhaps I identified him with the wounded men I had seen in the hospitals in World War II and had felt an urge to put my arms around and comfort, perhaps it only needed that to tip the scales in his favour, but I did take him in my arms that night, and next morning there was a patch of crimson on the sheet that made me feel very tender and loving indeed.

And happy, too. I had not felt so happy and fulfilled for years, nor been to bed with a man who so completely sensed my needs. The musical, *The King and I*, was the smash hit of the decade. It had a number of catchy tunes, one of which was: 'Getting to know you. Getting to learn all about you . . .' I sang it gaily as I went about the routine of the day.

Then the telephone rang. There was a woman's voice on the line that said: 'I'm Adrian Forbes's wife, Anita. He has told me all about you. I'm asking you to leave him alone. Our marriage hasn't been a happy one but since he came back from Australia, we've been trying to make a go of it. *Please* leave us alone.'

There was nothing to say but 'Of course! It means nothing to me. Good luck to you', and hang up the receiver.

Anger, astonishment, and the knowledge that I had fallen into the same old trap raged through me, and a strong feeling of disappointment also.

What a fool I had been! I should have known. And I did know. There had been no illusions about the kind of man he was. I had fallen for a smooth tongue and an accomplished cock. I knew! I knew! I knew! It was over. Done with. That bitch Aphrodite had played her last mean trick on me. To hell with her, she'd never get the chance again. Thank God I'd kept my mouth shut and told nobody, not even my closest friend, about the new interest in my life. Best to pretend it had never happened and get on with what I had to do.

Guido had once remarked that 'one of the best things about you is your inability to hold your anger'. And it was that way with Adrian Forbes. I suffered no sense of loss, only a feeling of contempt, and when he appeared again, without warning, several months later, it was mainly curiosity that prompted me to tell him to come in. How did he have the gall to confront me again? What excuse did he have for his despicable behaviour?

He put up a poor case in his defence. I listened and showed no emotion. In fact, I must have resembled my Aunt Belle to a remarkable degree, and could feel the set lines of her disapproval steal over my face as he floundered and stammered and finally gave up.

It was then well after ten o'clock. He had to catch a train from Charing Cross and rang for a taxi to be told that the chance of getting one was slim because the fog was so thick that even the taxi drivers had gone home. Incredulous, I threw back the curtains and looked into a solid wall of yellow fog. It was impossible to see for more than a few inches.

'You see,' said a triumphant voice behind me. 'You'll have to let me stay the night.'

'I'm damned if you will! I'll drive you to the station.'

'In this fog!'

'Either that or you sleep in the street.'

We got as far as Regent's Park and when I found that I was driving on the wrong side of the road and staring into the headlights of an approaching car, I had to admit defeat. Even that short distance, groping my way through that evil yellow wall, had taken so much time that the last train had gone, so there was nothing to be done but turn around and grope my way back home again.

Why didn't I tell him to get out while we were still in Regent's Park? My anger had cooled, that's why. The brief drive had been accompanied by so much peril that I could think of nothing else. Also, shared danger had forged a kind of bond between us. I had had to call on him for help and he had leaned out the open door and endeavoured to direct me, called out warnings when some stationary vehicle had loomed ahead, or when I was in danger of driving straight into one of the ornamental lakes. So when we finally reached Fitzjohn's Avenue my knees were so weak I could scarcely stand and I had no will to protest when he followed me inside. Nor when he followed me to bed. There was a fatalistic feeling. I had done my best to send him away, but the fog had defeated me.

Four days later there were symptoms that alarmed me. It could not possibly be, I told myself, and the initial wave of panic subsided. But the pain did not diminish and panic returned.

I could not bring myself to face my usual GP, who was also a good friend, but sought one I did not know. He listened gravely while I told him about the fog and about my fears.

'I shouldn't worry too much if I were you,' he said. 'Since the discovery of penicillin venereal disease is practically wiped out. Still, it's better to make sure. I think you'd better go to the clinic at University College Hospital. I'll give you a letter to the man in charge.'

University College Hospital in London is one of the world's great teaching hospitals and I knew that there I would receive a verdict that was indisputable, so it was with a sick feeling at the pit of my stomach that I went down the flight of steps that led to the clinic in the basement of that gloomy building in Gower Street.

The claim that venereal disease had been practically wiped out seemed to be confirmed by the waiting-room I entered through a heavy wooden door. It was huge, dimly lit and depressing. Bare

175

wooden seats were ranged along the walls and, besides myself, only one huddled figure sat staring at the floor.

I did not have long to wait before I was beckoned into an inner room. A distinguished-looking man in a white coat swivelled his chair around to look at me as I came in. He was courtesy itself. Questioned me, read the letter of referral, made some entries on a form and told me to go into yet another room and prepare myself for an exhaustive examination. It was not a pleasant experience and I see no point in going into details here. When it was over, I was given a card with a number on it and told to come back in two days' time. Which I did, and was told that the tests were positive and that I was suffering from acute gonorrhoea.

It was not the first time in my life when tears seemed inadequate and a sense of stupefaction stifled thought.

'I wouldn't take it so hard if I were you,' said the man in the white coat. 'It's not much worse than a cold in the head these days.'

'You haven't got it,' I answered, and he looked at me as though, for the first time, he had seen a human being and not a number of a card.

It was a bleak February day. It was not raining but the streets were wet with the prevailing damp and a thin cold haze hung over everything. Somehow, I managed to find my way to where I had left the car, switched the engine on, put it into gear, and drove straight into a letterbox on the kerb. It was an unnecessary blow and I began to cry.

'Do you need any help?' asked a voice. I shook my head, backed away from the kerb and, with tears still pouring down my cheeks, managed to weave my way through the peak-hour traffic to the haven of Fitzjohn's Avenue.

The penicillin did its work, and in a few days' time the symptoms abated and I was, to all appearances, cured. But the cure was superficial. I was tortured by a feeling of being unclean, of having been defiled. I hated myself—above all, I hated Adrian Forbes. If I could have done him some terrible physical injury,

I would have done so. All I could do was write him a letter, a violent, hysterical letter that was proof of a disordered mind. Before very long the answer came. I had expected remorse, even a degree of sympathy, instead of which he categorically denied all my accusations and enclosed a letter signed by his physician which said:

'My patient shows no symptoms of venereal disease in any of its forms, nor of ever having done so.'

I showed the letter to the man in the London clinic. 'There's been some mistake,' I said. 'You've got my slides mixed up with somebody else's.'

He looked startled and made a hasty search through the cards in a filing cabinet.

'No, I'm sorry,' he said. 'There's been no mistake and, regardless of what the letter says, I've no doubt in my mind about where your infection came from.'

'Is there any other way?'

'None whatever! All this talk about lavatory seats and dirty towels is utter nonsense. And if, as you say, he was the only man, there's your answer.'

This was said in an ambiguous tone, and left me with the feeling that perhaps he doubted Adrian really was 'the only man'. He was certainly going to be the last man! Never, as long as I lived, would any man make love to me again. The mere thought filled me with a feeling of revulsion.

Adrian's wife came to see me. She was a handsome, intelligent woman that I was disposed to like. She was genuinely sorry for me and expressed her sympathy, nevertheless supported her husband's claim of being blameless.

'I would have known,' she said. 'Adrian hides nothing from me.'

Not even his infidelities!

The attempt to patch up the marriage had failed, I learned, and Adrian had been involved with a woman in London, about which he kept her fully informed. She was also aware that when it had come to an end, he remembered me and thought he would see if he still found me attractive enough to go to bed with. This met with her approval as she, meanwhile, had formed an attachment of her own and did not want it to be disturbed.

'I thought we might make it a foursome,' she said as though planning a game of bridge. 'Adrian really likes you. He did from the time he met you in Sydney. Why not let bygones be bygones? Come down to Henley for the weekend and sort things out. You can bring Gilda if you like. Mark, my son, is just about her age. Maybe they could amuse each other too.'

I was too dumbfounded to speak, but recovered my wits and said I did not think that it was a good idea, and we parted with mutual expressions of goodwill.

She would have been amazed if I had told her that her proposition filled me with disgust, or that Adrian was the last man on earth with whom I would have anything to do. What was all the fuss about? she would have asked. What had happened to me was just bad luck and might have happened to anyone.

But I was unable to treat it so casually. To me, it was the ultimate degradation and plunged me into a mood of black depression that I was not able to shake off.

I was seeing myself through my Aunt Belle's eyes and could clearly recall the look of horror on her face when I told her the man to whom I was married had come back from Kalgoorlie with the same scourge that had now struck me. How pitiless I had been when he knelt at my side and pleaded for understanding.

'Don't be too hard on your poor old husband,' he had said, and I had thrust him aside and reviled him. Was this ordeal my punishment?

With these and other thoughts I tormented myself to the brink of a nervous collapse, but again sound commonsense came to my aid and I realised that I must get away from everything that reminded me of the night of the yellow fog and the clinic in the basement of the London hospital.

I needed somewhere that was clean and fresh and wholesome, where I could begin to forget. The name of that place was Sarre.

The friendship with Teddy and Peggy Cleven that had begun

in the Embassy Theatre days had endured and on a number of occasions I had spent a weekend with them in Kent. The club they managed was owned by a retired wing-commander, known as the Wingco, who took exception to the fact that Peg fell pregnant again and told Teddy that 'if they were going to breed like rabbits, they had better do it somewhere else'.

Not surprisingly, Teddy took exception to *that*, went to see his bank manager, got a sympathetic hearing, and bought a rather neglected two-storey house in Sarre, a tiny village not more than two miles away from the Wing-Commander's club. They called it Sarre Court, and took almost all of Wingco's patrons with them. Sarre Court was a success from the moment it first opened its hospitable doors.

It was to this cheerful, bustling place that I went in search of a cure for my emotional ills, and I could not have found a better one. There were constant comings and goings, noise and laughter, and an air of optimism that hung about the place like an aura.

London seemed far away, and no-one had time to question why I had come to live at Sarre, or why I went off to my room each night instead of joining the convivial group that lingered round the bar when all the more sober-minded guests had gone, and Teddy would close the shutters, draw the curtains, switch off the outside lights, and the serious business of the night commenced.

An astonishing amount of alcohol was consumed, which was an additional reason for taking refuge in my room, apart from an instinctive dislike of getting drunk and stupid. I was finding it increasingly difficult to keep up the supply of scripts for Hulton Press and knew that a hangover in the morning would bring an end of inspiration for the day. The bright ideas that had once flowed so easily from my pen were beginning to dry up, and I began to dread the thought of a mental block like the one I had had in 1951, when my mind had seized like an overheated engine until, finally, it had refused to function at all. It is the nightmare that all authors dread, and few of us are spared.

179

Each day became an agony. I would sit in front of the typewriter and stare at the blank page and pray that ideas would start to flow again. The more I worried, the worse the block became. I would go to bed at night and tell myself that my subconscious would get to work and I would wake up next day with my sanity restored. But my subsconscious refused to work and my mind was still a blank when I woke up.

Peg came into my room one day and found me in despair. The floor was littered with discarded sheets of paper, and I was in tears.

'Bettykins! What on earth is the matter?' she asked.

For a moment, I was tempted to tell her the truth, to unburden myself of my miserable secret and perhaps get rid of the sense of defilement that was haunting me. But the thought of the expression of disgust that would come over her pretty face prevented me, so I dried my eyes, told her it was nothing and that I would be down to lunch as usual.

Canterbury is only a few miles away from Sarre. I loved the picturesque old town with its narrow streets, quaint old houses and especially the magnificent cathedral that dominates them all. It became a symbol to me of all that is best and noblest in man and helped restore my belief that he is capable of the sublime as well as the profane.

There is a small very lovely chapel in the north-west transept of which I was particularly fond. It is dedicated to the memory of that 'troublesome priest', Thomas a'Becket, Archbishop of Canterbury, who had dared oppose his king and died on the altar steps for refusing to bow to the royal will. From time to time a late afternoon service would be held there and, unbeliever though I was, I felt a sense of peace as I bowed my head and murmured the responses while the shadows gathered among the soaring arches and the western sun turned the stained glass windows into flaming blue and crimson jewels

I went there that afternoon and found a service in progress. Only a handful of people were there and I took a seat as quietly as I could and waited till the beautifully modulated voice of the officiating priest pronounced the benediction and the worshippers filed out. The priest had silver hair and a fine spiritual face that reminded me of Kester, and I felt that I could talk to him. Canterbury Cathedral is High Church, and confessions are regularly heard, so he would not be shocked at what I had to tell him, the expression on his face would not change.

He seemed surprised when he emerged from somewhere behind the altar and saw me sitting there alone. Coming slowly down the aisle, he paused beside my chair.

'Did you wish to talk to me?' he asked.

Here was my moment, but I let it pass, unable to bring myself to begin.

'Are you in trouble?' the gentle voice went on.

'Yes.' Tears came easily those days and I began to cry.

He took a seat at my side and waited till I grew calm. 'Would you like to tell me what it is?'

'I'm not able to work. I can't think any more, and I'll lose my job.'

I did not intend to say that, the words were irrelevant, absurd, and I was ashamed of them.

'What kind of work do you do?'

'I'm a writer. I write adventure stories for boys and girls.' This took him by surprise.

'I see.'

I dried my eyes. 'It isn't only that . . .' He glanced at his watch.

'Suppose you come and see me some other time. I have an appointment at six o'clock.'

I said I would like that and he told me who he was and where to come in two days' time. He was the dean of the cathedral and lived in one of the quaint old houses I so admired.

I went at the appointed time, and find it difficult to describe the frame of mind that I was in. The black mood of my depression had passed and I was starting to write again. What, then, had I come to say to this saintly-looking man? Had I come to cast my burden on the Lord and ask for His forgiveness?

The time for that had passed. I had been ripe for redemption

181

in Thomas a' Becket's chapel but the Dean's appointment at six o'clock had intervened. Perhaps the Lord had not been ready to receive me then; would He be waiting for me in the Deanery that afternoon? I rather doubted it, but rang the bell and waited to be let in.

The Dean was waiting for me in his pleasant book-lined room. He got up to welcome me and told me to sit on an uncomfortable wooden chair while he resumed his seat behind a mahogany desk and placed the tips of his beautiful white fingers together in a way that reminded me of Albrecht Durer's famous engraving. After a few preliminary questions such as my name, marital status and where I had come from, he closed his eyes and began a long monologue.

He used beautiful, poetic words that had a soothing effect and which I took to be a form of prayer, but went on overlong, I thought, and I wondered when he would turn his attention to me. But the melodious voice went on, and by the time he opened his eyes and asked what it was that I had come about, I had lost all wish to tell him. Instead, I remained evasive, told him I had been ill and had come to Sarre to recuperate, had been feeling low when I spoke to him in Thomas a' Becket's shrine, but it had been a passing mood and I now felt very much better.

He expressed his pleasure at hearing that, said I was welcome to come any time I felt in need of help, and that he would conduct a special service in the crypt of the cathedral in a few day's time which I might like to attend. Then the interview was over.

The crypt is a gloomy place, full of ghosts and brooding shadows that lurk between massive pillars that support the great cathedral towering above it. It was there that the repentant king, Henry II, had crawled across the floor on his bare knees and lashed himself until his blood had stained the altar steps as Thomas a' Becket's had done. There were no candles on the altar, no flowers, no embroidered altar cloths, only a single crucifix on the bare stone.

The dean appeared and took his place among the shadows and the small assembly bowed their heads as the beautifully modulated voice recited a brief prayer and then began his address. It was a repetition of the monologue that I had listened to in his book-lined room. I could scarcely credit my ears. Was it a set piece, one among many, that he employed as the need arose, or was he rehearsing his lines as any actor would do?

Once or twice, I thought he looked in my direction, but I could not be sure as the light was very dim. When the final blessing had been pronounced and the service was at an end, I followed the assembled few up the flight of stairs to where the man of God stood waiting to say the customary words of greeting and farewell. I was among the last and he took my hand and looked at me in a slightly puzzled manner.

'Haven't we met before?' he said.

I shook my head and said I didn't think we had.

I drove back to Sarre in a distinctly lightened mood. Instead of feeling hurt and angry at the dean's forgetfulness, I was amused. Principally at myself. Once again, I had fallen for a soft voice and a handsome face.

'Roland, Roland, you're a hopeless case,' I told myself, and when I got back to Sarre went into the bar and ordered a Bloody Mary before I changed for dinner.

CHAPTER 20

Although I had been disappointed in the dean and felt I had been given a stone instead of the sacramental bread I had been hoping for, my black depression lifted and there were no more tears. Instead, I started to enjoy life with the Clevens, which does not mean that I joined the heavy drinkers in the bar. I found pleasure in simpler things such as a game of golf, a harmless game of bridge with Peg's mother and her two cronies in the village, or knitting woolly garments when Peg's third baby was on the way. All very innocent, but I did not find it boring— there had been too much drama in my life, too much excitement, and I was glad of a change.

Best of all, I loved to sit before a fire and gossip with Peg's mother, known to everyone as Granny Dickon. Despite the difference in our ages we became firm friends, and the hours spent with her bring back some of the happiest memories of Sarre. She was a spritely old lady with a sense of humour and a strong will of her own and was slightly surprised at finding herself, in her old age, living in such an unorthodox atmosphere as the one that permeated Sarre Court. She thought the patrons, by and large, were a godless lot, and commended me because I showed no inclination to linger round the bar. And I sometimes wondered what her response would be if I told her just why I had come to Sarre!

We had much in common. She told me about her life on a Shropshire farm while I told her about my grandfather's farm in faraway Australia. She came from sturdy English yeoman stock, I from Northern Irish Protestants and a deep love of the land ran in our blood and made us kin. I had married at nineteen and had a son who died when he was seven; she had married quite late in life and surprised herself by having three children in quick succession, a boy and two girls, the youngest of whom was Peg.

She told an amusing tale of taking Peg with her to Brussels and how the perky little redhead had bewitched the young men.

'I practically had to beat them off with a broom,' was her way of describing the scene. 'But Teddy was not to be put off. He'd set his heart on Peg and won.' She might have added that Peg had set her heart on Teddy and that opposition on her mother's part was useless. It was a simple, uncomplicated, very beautiful story of young love and did much to restore my faith in the human race.

Restored to a rational state of mind, I no longer felt a wish to isolate myself, began to frequent the bar, found friends who were congenial and shared with them the in-house jokes. Once, in a reckless moment, I agreed to go on one of their nocturnal treasure-hunts, which I had been assured I would enjoy. These mad escapades took place at a time when it was hoped that all right-minded people would be at home in bed, leaving the roads free of traffic so that the 'huntsmen' could drive wildly along the narrow, winding roads of Kent in search of the so-called treasure, which had been concealed in some unlikely place and must be found with the aid of certain clues. I sat in the back of a souped-up Morris Minor, which was driven by the son of the local doctor, and his cousin who acted as navigator. They had spent the day tuning the engine and I hoped they had paid some attention to its brakes as well. There was a thin drizzle of rain and a suggestion of future fog which did nothing to calm my nerves.

The first clue led us to a cemetery in St Nicholas-at-Wade, where we had to find a tombstone in the north-east corner and decipher the inscription and note the date on which the last occupant had been buried before racing off to find an equally unlikely object hidden in a ditch. There were fully twenty other contestants for the prize, and the probability of a crash increased at every turn. We solved the next two clues and then met with a check. We were told to find a 'cromlech' in a field whose whereabouts were only vaguely indicated.

'What the hell is a cromlech?' the driver enquired. Luckily, the navigator had brought a dictionary and, with the aid of an electric torch, we learnt that a cromlech is 'a circle of upright prehistoric stones, or megalithic tomb of Welsh origin, rarely seen in Britain.'

'Jesus, don't say we've got to go to Wales!' the navigator exclaimed.

'No, you idiot, I know where it is,' the driver said, and off we went with a screech of tyres and finally reached a cul-de-sac which was already choked with cars that had preceded us.

The drizzle had increased to a steady downpour and I declined to join them as they scrambled through the hedge and raced off across the sodden field to find the prehistoric ring of stones or megalithic tomb that had somehow strayed from Wales. We were now far back in the field and, much to my relief, the navigator missed a turn and we got lost. After some heated argument it was decided to admit defeat and make our way back to Sarre, a stiff whisky and a warm bed and, on my part, a resolve never to indulge in such an exercise in lunacy again.

So, there was no lack of 'cakes and ale' at Sarre Court, and the two years there were happy, peaceful years and might have continued indefinitely had not Gilda decided to go back to Australia. This was something I had never reckoned on, and meant a total readjustment of my life.

While I had been at Sarre she had been sharing the flat in Regent's Park with Jean Crouch, the editress of *Girl*, and her husband, James, the psychiatrist. In the light of what I have said about James it may seem an odd sort of place in which to leave her, but lysergic acid, or LSD as it is now known, did not have the evil reputation that it has today. Apart from a few *cognoscenti* such as James, it was relatively unknown and while I had observed its effect on Jean with some concern, I did not dream that I was exposing my daughter to any sort of danger. Nor was I. James confined his experiments to his wife. Gilda went off to her job in the New South Wales Agent-General's office in the Strand each morning, Jean continued to edit *Girl*, and the Siamese cats went on with their incestuous life as before.

The cats were one of the reasons why Gilda was granted the privilege of living in Regent's Park. Jean and James had a rustic cottage in Devon and liked to spend a few days there from time to time. The cats presented a problem, as they either had to take them with them or leave them to fend for themselves, but with Gilda on hand to feed them their Kit-e-kat and empty their reeking sand trays down the lavatory, they could go away with an easy mind. When they were away, I would go to London and stay with her; when they were in residence, she would come for a weekend at Sarre. It was an admirable arrangement which suited all of us.

Then Gilda met a young man called Jonathan and fell in love with him. This was not surprising as she had grown into a lovely girl and was twenty years of age. There had been some minor affairs, but Jonathan was the first to whom she had given her young heart. He was the spoilt only son of adoring parents, especially his mother, and treated her rather casually, which did not dampen her ardour in the least, and when he went back to Australia she was inconsolable, though there were at least two other young men I thought would be a distinct improvement on the absent Jonathan. But she found fault with both of them, one because he trod on her toes when he danced with her, the other because he had clammy hands.

Against such flimsy objections there was no point in arguing, so I told her she had better go out to Australia and either marry Jonathan or forget him, a suggestion she accepted with alacrity.

She had never been really happy in England, had never been able to adjust herself to the new life or overcome her feeling of being an outsider, and as it was now seven years since the *Cyrenia* had sailed, it seemed futile to hope that she would change. But I was not going with her. I loved England and, especially, London, so would stay there and hope that she would find out her mistake, both with regard to Jonathan and to Australia, and beg to return.

The thought of parting with her was a severe wrench. She was due to sail in two months' time, so I said goodbye to Sarre and went back to London to have the last few weeks with her. My usual phenomenal luck in finding a pleasant place to live again asserted itself and I found a flat in Harley Street, W1. What impulse made me pause and read the notice in the window of a shop in Hampstead, I shall never know, but there it was, writ large in purple ink: TO LET. Furnished flat in Harley Street, for short term. Two ladies only. Must be fond of cats. £5.15 a week.

Unable to believe my eyes, I rushed for the nearest phone. A rather fruity voice told me that the flat was still available and that I could come to see it that afternoon.

It was in the basement, but was indeed in Harley Street. It was a little dark, perhaps, and in winter it would be very cold, but we would be gone by the time the frosts arrived, Gilda to Sydney and I . . . I did not yet know where. Meanwhile, it would suit us very well. There was a small walled garden at the back, which accounted for the need to be fond of cats. The lady with the fruity voice had two dilapidated tabbies who required access to the garden through the basement kitchen door.

Two months can pass very rapidly, and the last day came. I watched the ship cast off and the last coloured streamer flutter in the wind and then went back to Harley Street to sort out the chaos in the flat and to sort out my own life. The lady with the fruity voice came down in search of her cats and saw me staring at the litter of discarded clothes, torn up letters, and the unmade bed in what had been Gilda's room.

'Ah yes,' she said, 'they go away and leave you to your misery.'

She had never been very friendly, but in that moment we shared the common woe of women. She, too, had said goodbye to someone dearly loved and returned to an empty flat.

Once again, an unwanted liberation had been forced upon me. I was responsible to no-one and whatever follies I might commit, no-one would suffer but myself. But I had had enough of suffering, and hoped that the age of folly was behind me. The two years at Sarre had done nothing to alter my determination to have nothing more to do with men, and it had been less difficult than I had feared. The passions cool when one is over fifty years of age, but I still missed the companionship, the close affinity that I had known with Guido, and had never quite recovered from a sense of irreparable loss. In other words, I was lonely. To which there was only one cure.

My wild excesses in the past had been nothing less than a search for another Guido. I had almost succeeded once or twice. Alan Williamson seemed close to my ideal, but my thoughtless revelation of his unguarded remark about Norman Rydge and Ealing Studios had ruined all hopes of permanence there. Arthur Munday at Montsalvat had been another, I really thought I had found the solution there, but his allegiance to Justus Jorgensen was greater than his love for me and it was not in my nature to be second best. My hope had revived when I met Kester Berwick, but the presence of John Tasker had put an end to that. But John was no longer with him; he had found a younger, more congenial friend than the ageing man who had helped him when he had been a paperboy in Newcastle and had trouble with his speech. Now Kester was alone.

He still taught drama at the City Literary Institute but was growing restless and thinking of going to live in Greece.

'Why don't you come with me?' he said. 'Living is very cheap there and you can always earn a few drachmas by teaching English, which I intend to do.'

The idea appealed to me, as my early love of all things Greek had been increased by the time I had spent there in 1952, but there were obstacles in the way. One was my job with Hulton Press. I doubted if even so reasonable an editor as Marcus Morris would be in favour of my writing stories for *Girl* from so remote a point as an island in the Aegean, where Kester planned to be. The mail was bound to be unreliable. In addition, a new avenue had recently opened up for me. I had been asked to write a book, a modest enough affair, but one of a series for children between the ages of eight and twelve who, to date, had been rather overlooked and for whom the prestigious Bodley Head was anxious to cater.

It was an opportunity not to be missed. A book, however modest, was an advance on the soap operas and cartoon strips that had been my sole literary achievements since the brief glory of *The Touch of Silk* more than thirty years ago. A book was something permanent, something I could hold in my hands and admire. I would no longer feel ashamed when somebody asked me what sort of things did I write. I had already made a start on *The Forbidden Bridge* and felt it was going well, so I told Kester I wanted to remain in London until it was finished and then I would think about joining him in Greece.

It took longer than I thought, as there was the business of editing and rewriting certain passages, but finally The Bodley Head was satisfied and a contract signed. A writer's first contract with a publisher is a unique experience, never quite repeated, and when I walked down Floral Street in Covent Garden with the precious document in my hand, I could not have been more elated if I had been awarded the Booker Prize.

There had also been the hint of a commission to write a sequel to *The Forbidden Bridge*, which meant the beginning of a new career. So, when Marcus Morris agreed that the Aegean was just a little too far away from Fleet Street, I said goodbye to *Girl* and *Swift*, though not without regret. They had been part of my life for almost seven years, and had made it possible for me to live in London, to see the marvels of Europe, and I was grateful for that. The loss of income did not trouble me, as my share in my Aunt Belle's estate had steadily increased and would now enable me to live in Greece without having to teach English.

Kester was now living on Lesbos, Sappho's island, and wrote enthusiastic accounts of the island's beauty, its peaceful way of life and the charm of the Greek people.

'What is keeping you in London?' he wrote. 'You could have no more ideal place in which to write your books than Lesbos.'

An island in the Aegean is the secret dream of almost every writer, so why did I hesitate? I had read Charmian Clift's book, *Peel Me a Lotus*, which gave an account of her life on the island of Hydra with her husband, George; a tale of boredom, disillusion and disintegration that filled me with foreboding. Might I also share their fate? But what was the alternative? Sarre Court, London, Australia? The thought of the latter had already occurred to me, as I was missing Gilda rather badly, but being unsure of the welcome I would receive, I had put it out of my mind. I was then living in Earls Court, as I wanted to see if my fellow Australians were as outlandish as they were reputed to be. The answer was mainly negative, but I still felt no wish to spend the remainder of my life with them. Maybe, in a few years time . . . Meanwhile, there was Lesbos.

It was towards the end of March before I had finally packed up and boarded the Channel steamer at Dover. It was a stormy crossing. We were late in reaching Calais, and the train to Paris had been delayed for twenty minutes, so there was no time for an orderly transition from one to the other, but a mad scramble instead. I had a large tin trunk that was full of books, a smaller one full of clothes, and an overnight bag that was new and that I set special store by. Instead of being put in the luggage van, they were all slung in after me just as the train began to move, and effectively blocked the entrance should anybody attempt to follow.

I looked at them with a sense of fatalism. For better or for worse, they would have to remain until we got to Paris. I staggered along the corridor in search of the seat I had so hopefully reserved. A usurper had taken possession of it and refused to be dislodged, and I was resigning myself to an uncomfortable two hours when a nice young man got up and insisted that I have his seat. He was French and spoke perfect English and appeared not to mind having to stand all the way to the Gare du Nord.

There a fresh crisis arose. The two trunks were still where I had left them but the overnight bag had gone. Also, the trunks were blocking the exit so an exasperated guard heaved them onto the platform to be dealt with as best I could. There was not a porter to be seen; they were either on strike or had been grabbed by the other passengers, and I had to get those heavy trunks onto another platform before the train to Athens left in twenty minutes' time. Then French chivalry once more came to my aid. The nice young man who had given me his seat saw my distress, found a trolley somewhere, hoisted the trunks on board and dragged them onto the other platform, and with five minutes to spare, saw me safely onto the Orient Express.

Until I saw Vienna, Budapest, Athens, Istanbul and other exotic cities written on the outside of the carriages, I had no idea that the ticket I had bought in London entitled me to a *wagon-lit* on this most fabulous of trains, so I thanked my young knight-errant, kissed him on the cheek and settled back to enjoy a three-day journey without make-up, nightdress, or a brush and comb. There had been no time to put the troublesome trunks in the luggage van, so they shared the *wagon-lit* with me and caused the steward some concern. He did not volunteer to shift them, however, and they gave no further trouble until we got to Athens.

I had planned to stay at the New Angleterre hotel, but it had been demolished to make way for the glittering glass and concrete monstrosity that housed the American Express. Similar changes had taken place elsewhere, but the *evzones* still went through their complicated ritual before the Royal Palace, and the Parthenon still hung suspended in the sky, and there was souvlaki and *bouzouki* music in the Plaka. But an empty chair faced me across the table, a reminder of my solitary state. Was that going to change? I wondered. Would there be a familiar face on the far side of the table in future? It was that hope that had brought me to Greece and buoyed me up during the overnight voyage to Lesbos.

There was a violent storm in the night, and the little ship tossed wildly in the gale, but the wind died in the morning, and by the time Lesbos appeared on the horizon the Aegean was its usual celestial blue, the sun shone brightly on the island's dramatic skyline and the endless little coves and inlets along its rocky coast. Mytilini, the island capital, came into view and we nosed our way through the narrow gap in the mole that protects the little harbour from the wind and waves. The captain ordered three blasts on the siren to announce our safe arrival, and the people on the quay began to shout and wave their handkerchiefs, plainly relieved to see us, as we were three hours late. Kester was there to greet me and put my doubts at rest by his obvious pleasure at seeing me and the warmth of his embrace.

Mytilini was a surprise. I had not been prepared for its size, for the shops, the hotels and the handsome residences built on the slope of the hill that rose above the town, the Byzantine church with its cupolas, or the Genoese fortress crowning the crest of the hill. This was no village settlement but a handsome city. Why had Kester not told me about it in his letters? Kester lived in Molyvos, a village on the other side of the island and there was a three-hour drive over an atrocious road before we finally arrived there.

Because of the late arrival of the boat, there was barely time to bundle the luggage into a taxi and drive to the square where all the island buses set out in the early afternoon. The bus to Molyvos had delayed its departure for my sake and the driver started up the engine when he saw us coming. Another man leapt out and seized my luggage and hoisted it onto the roof, Kester paid the taxi driver, and we were on our way. The bus was crowded to capacity and there was a deal of shuffling and shifting before a few inches were found for me on the end of a seat and a folding stool for Kester in the aisle.

We went honking through the narrow streets. Men with donkeys, stray hens and lean dogs scattered before us; women stood in doorways watching us go past; a black-robed priest leaped nimbly onto the footpath, scowling at us as he did so. The driver waved his hand apologetically, the priest responded and we roared on once more in a state of grace. Soon we were clear of the town and began the long climb through the hills and the man beside me opened the bundle on his lap, took out a loaf of bread, broke off a piece and handed it to me. It was the ancient traditional way of welcoming a stranger. He did not have the customary salt, but it tasted none the less delicious because of that. We smiled at each other and he said '*chairete*' (greetings).

Then a young man in the back began to play on his guitar,

singing as he did so. Soon everyone joined in and we lurched along to the harsh music of Greek folk songs, through the olive groves, past the Gulf of Yhera, climbing steadily upwards till the grey-green olive groves were replaced by shaggy mountain pines.

Lesbos is not the barren, sun-blasted island that so many of the Aegean islands are, but is known as a 'green island' because of its forests and the streams that laugh and gurgle down the mountain side and its profusion of flowers: cyclamen, anemones, crocuses, and asphodel, said to be the flowers of the Underworld. Kester had spoken truly when he said that it was perhaps the most beautiful island of them all.

The sun grew hotter, the road grew worse, we left the pine forests behind and drove through mountain passes as stark and treeless as a Doré landscape. The singing ceased, the man put away his guitar and the driver switched on the radio, blasting our ears with horrid sound while the old bus rocked and swayed and the springs groaned a protest at being asked to follow the impossible road. Finally, we reached the summit, paused to allow the panting engine to cool down and then began the long descent, once more through pines, olive groves and then the maize fields and the vegetable gardens of the fertile plains. The old bus shook and rocked like a horse that sniffs the stables when nearing home.

'There it is,' cried Kester. 'There's Molyvos!'

And there, ahead of us, it was. A cluster of stone houses clung like limpets to the side of a steeply rising hill, their walls so white they dazzled the eyes, crowned like Mytilini by the ruins of an ancient fortress. There was a small, snug harbour where fishing boats were moored, and everywhere the peerless blue of the Aegean. Five more minutes and we had arrived, the old bus dripping oil and waves of vapour rising from its throbbing heart. A group of men and boys stood awaiting our arrival in the shade of an enormous walnut tree. One of them detached himself and came forward as Kester helped me onto the ground.

'This is Helmut,' Kester said. 'He is teaching German here, I think I mentioned him in one of my letters.'

He may have done so, but I did not remember. One look at Helmut's stolid Teutonic face reassured me. In no way whatever did he resemble the handsome John.

My first night in Molyvos was spent in its one primitive hotel. The room was simple in the extreme and had a bed, a table and an earthern pitcher standing in a basin on the windowsill, but beyond that window was a view that the Grande Bretagne in Athens could not provide. We ate that night at Kosta's taverna and had *kalamari* and *souvlaki* with a bottle of retsina, for which Kosta refused to be paid. I was no longer facing an empty chair on the other side of the table. A new life had begun.

Next morning I was taken to see a room in one of the square white houses on the outskirts of the town. Kester told me not to take the first room that I saw, as there were others to be had, but it was a room of shining whiteness with bright rugs on the floor and the tang of the sea drifting through its open windows. Below it was the port with its blue and red and yellow fishing boats, the traditional *caiques*, and the coast of Turkey, a smudge of blue, on the horizon. I looked no further—this was the place of my dreams, where I was going to live and write great books. The rent was 450 drachmas a month, which when converted into English currency, amounted to 27s 6d a week.

CHAPTER 21

'Tomorrow is "cleansing Monday",' Kester announced soon after I arrived 'and you're invited to a picnic.'

'What on earth is "cleansing Monday"?' I wanted to know.

'It marks the beginning of Lent, so all the houses are scrubbed and cleaned and the men and the children go out for the day and leave the women to it. We've been invited to go to Eftarloo with my landlord and his family.'

Kester had two rooms in a fine old Turkish house which was in a state of advanced decay, but it had a view that almost equalled mine, and a vine-covered trellis and fig trees laden with fruit; his landlord and his family occupied the lower floor and took a keen interest in everything Kester did. Hence the invitation to picnic at Eftarloo. But the car refused to start and there were apologies and mutual expressions of regret, and Kester and I decided we would walk. Helmut promised to join us later on, but must have changed his mind as he did not appear.

Every house we passed was buzzing with activity. Furniture was being shifted out from walls, brooms and scrubbing brushes were scouring floors and paintwork, and from every upper window rugs were being shaken free of dust, and mattresses and blankets aired in the warm spring sun. Husbands, grandmas, children and surplus males had been banished for the day and would not return until the frenzy had abated and peace restored. Such was cleansing Monday.

Kester had assured me that Eftarloo was within easy walking distance of Molyvos, but we had not gone very far before it became apparent that the walk would be neither easy nor short. We had to cross a saddle in the hills at least three kilometres away and the road was strewn with stones. I was beginning to regret my flimsy shoes when we were overtaken by a string of donkeys and three men. They must have read my thoughts as they stopped and greeted us and asked if we would like to ride. Nothing could have pleased me better, and in no time I was hoisted onto the back of one of the pretty little beasts and drumming my heels against its ribs in the traditional donkey-rider's way. The men resumed their steady lope along the road and asked the usual questions. Who were we, where did we come from, and why had we come to Molyvos? In return we were told that they came from a village high up in the mountains and sold firewood in Molyvos and produce from their farms. When the Germans had occupied the island in the last war one of them had crossed to Turkey in a caique and in some extraordinary fashion found his way to Egypt, where he had driven a truck for the Australian army. He rolled up the leg of his trousers and showed us the wound he had received while doing so. All this came out when he heard that we were from Australia and we greeted each other like long-lost brothers.

Eftarloo was totally deserted. It is a tiny beach between two headlands that kept out the wind, so we sat on the sand with our backs against a boulder and ate our lunch with a feeling of great content. We talked of old friends far away, of things we had done and seen and other small inconsequential matters, or sat drowsing in the sun, saying nothing at all. Later, we explored the deserted houses built along the shore. They were summer residences, *koolas*, and belonged to the prosperous citizens of Mytilini and a few from Molyvos, of whom Kester's landlord was one. They were simple to the point of austerity, but had fig and walnut trees and vine-covered trellises with wooden seats and tables underneath where it would be very pleasant to sit and drink on a summer evening.

At one end of the beach there was a bath-house, a relic of the years of Turkish occupation, where a hot spring bubbled out of the earth, spilled out of the rough stone bath and lost itself in the sea. I dipped my hand in the water and found it was too hot so took off my shoes and waded into the Aegean and found it had been warmed for quite some distance from the shore by this strange tributary from the hot heart of the earth.

We walked back to Molyvos as the sun was going down and came across some shepherds leading home their flock of goats and longhaired sheep. They were gnarled, weatherbeaten men and their faces were scored by years of bitter toil and hardship. Each one smiled and called a cheery '*chairete*' as we went past, the tinkle of the sheep-bells making fairy music in the evening air.

A violent storm blew up that night and reminded me that Lesbos was one of the Aeolian Isles and that the wind that rattled the shutters and threatened to dislodge the tiles was the same kind of wind that had blown Ulysses off-course two thousand years ago. I remembered that Troy was not so far away, and planned to visit it quite soon. I felt that I was living in a dream. I had been told to stay indoors, as it was not safe to walk along the street, but the storm abated as the sun went down and I found my way through broken tiles and the fallen branches of trees to where Helmut and Kester were waiting in Kosta's taverna, where we had planned to have our evening meal.

Kosta's taverna was the social centre of the town. There one met the mayor, the priest and the schoolmaster, as well as the fishermen, the muleteers and the men who sold wood from the mountains. It was there that I met Yannis, the poor, lost man. Yannis had the saddest eyes that I had ever seen, and his story was doubly affecting because his misfortunes began in Australia. As so many able-bodied Greeks had done, he had gone there in search of a new and better life, but he had been sent to work in Port Pirie, one of the most unlovely and depressing places any man could be consigned to. Isolation, loneliness and the slow corrosion of despair had cracked his mind, and after some months in a psychiatric ward in Adelaide he had been declared incurable and transported back to Greece.

His mind was still unhinged, but he was harmless enough. He liked to come and sit with us, not saying very much but staring unseeingly ahead, sometimes accepting a glass of *ouzo* or a plate of food. It was not easy to make conversation.

'Are you glad to be back in Molyvos?' I asked one time.

'What is there to be glad about?'

'You're back home, among your own people. There's the beauty and the sunlight.'

He looked at me with those haunted, unhappy eyes. 'Ah yes,' he said. 'In Greece there's everything but work.'

One night, he seemed unusually on edge and kept glancing out the door. A powerful-looking man came in and spoke to him—just a few low words, but Yannis understood. Jumping to his feet, he followed him out the door, leaving a half-smoked cigarette to smoulder in a saucer, his glass of *ouzo* undrunk. We received evasive answers when we asked about him.

'He's being taken away,' they said. 'There have been complaints about him. He frightens the children and makes a nuisance of himself. He'd create a bad impression when the summer visitors arrive.'

Yannis was not the only one in Molyvos who had been touched by tragedy. There was the woman whose husband had been murdered one night as he came home from Petra, a village not far away from Molyvos. It was a *crime passionel* performed by the brothers of a girl he had seduced. His widow, in addition to wearing the mandatory mourning for the remainder of her life, closed the shutters of her house, had it painted black, went inside and closed the doors and was never seen in the *agora* again.

There was also the grey-haired woman sitting alone in a tiny room, hour after hour, day after day, staring sightlessly ahead, with no change of expression on her face. She had a handsome though ravaged face, the brow wide, the mouth firm, whisps of hair straggling on each side. Once I saw the village priest with her, but never anybody else.

I asked about her but received evasive answers. She was an 'evil woman, very, very bad,' was the most I heard. Kester had heard vague stories, though. She had been a schoolteacher, a talented and intelligent woman, who had fraternised with the Germans during the occupation. Even worse than that, she had been guilty of helping a poor, distracted girl, who had 'fraternised' too closely, to abort her unwanted child. How much truth there was in that one could not say, but there she sat, day after day, until, like poor Yannis, she was spirited away before the summer visitors arrived.

Those summer visitors were, indirectly, the cause of my leaving Molyvos and going to live in Mytilini.

Themistocles, my landlord, and Ephstratea, his wife, had started to act strangely; they were not as cordial and anxious to please as they had been before, and matters came to a head when I invited Kester and Helmut to come and have a home-cooked meal with me. I planned to give them Irish stew. It had to be a stew, because there was only a primus stove and one aluminium pot in a corner of my room. Ephstratea kept poking her head in the door while the stew was being cooked, and from the expression on her face it was plain that she disapproved of what was going on.

While the meal was in progress, Themistocles burst in, glared at the three of us, and left without a word.

'Does he think we're having an orgy?' Helmut said.

'They're upset at Betty for having two men in her room,' Kester said.,

'Better than having one,' said I.

Next morning there were scowls and black looks, and when I came back from the *agora* that afternoon, the stove and the saucepan had been removed and the pretty woven rugs that I so admired were no longer on the floor. There was the bed, a chair, and the bare table and nothing else. 'Them' and 'Eff', as they were facetiously known by us three 'foreigners', spoke hardly any English, I very little Greek, so Kester had to intervene. He came back looking rather grave.

'They want you to go,' he said. When I demanded to know why he said: 'It's because of the tourist season. They've been offered a higher rent.'

'Why didn't they say? I'd have paid them anything in reason.'

'It isn't only that. A woman by herself is looked on with suspicion. Now, don't get upset! They are simple people here and women don't go about by themselves . . .'

'Or have men in their rooms at night!'

'That's it, I guess.'

'Let them have their room. I'll find one somewhere else.'

But where? For some undisclosed reason, rooms in Molyvos were unobtainable. Neither was there a house, though shuttered windows and an air of neglect suggested that some were unoccupied.

Yes, they were empty, I was told, but the owner lived in Athens and was due to arrive in Molyvos any day, or the house had already been let and was unavailable. It took me a while to realise that this was part of a conspiracy to drive me out of Molyvos. Greek women, widowed or single, rarely move out of their house unaccompanied by some member of their family, even when going to church. Never, under any circumstances, would she sit in a taverna and drink *ouzo* with a man who was not her husband, much less entertain him in her room. I was guilty of flouting all their moral codes, therefore judged to be a woman of doubtful character, setting a bad example, and it was best that I go.

Kester did his best to persuade me to stay, to be patient and to make allowances for different values. Once they got to know me and realised that our friendship was platonic, he said, their natural warmth and friendliness would assert itself and I would be accepted as a welcome addition to their little community. Kester never saw malice in anyone and always believed the best of them—even of me. He never saw me as I am: impatient, intolerant, on occasion ruthless. Nor did he suspect the real reason why I wanted to go away from Molyvos.

Greece is noted for its beautiful young men, and Molyvos is no exception. When one of them came and sat with us in the taverna Kester paid no more attention to me but devoted himself to the interloper, sometimes caressing his bare arm or laying a hand on his thigh, the female in me was outraged, and I had difficulty in suppressing my resentment. He must have wondered sometimes why I was suddenly silent or got up and walked away. I was jealous of the beautiful young men, and hated Kester for being what he was and preferring them to me.

But I did not tell him that. I did not want to hurt him, I did not want to see the look of distress on his face. I wanted to retain his friendship. So I said I thought I might enjoy living in Mytilini, where there were sure to be plenty of nice places to live. He could come and see me whenever he liked and could even stay overnight, as Mytilini was a far more worldly place than Molyvos and would not think any the worse of me. I still had a lot to learn about Greek mores.

CHAPTER 22

Mytilini had a number of houses and flats to let, and I settled on a neat two-storeyed villa on the fringes of the town. It seemed ideal: clean airy rooms, kitchen, bathroom, sun porch, sewerage, a garden enclosed by a high stone wall and within two hundred yards of the sea—all for a mere five pounds a month.

I unpacked my books, hung a few pictures on the wall, got out the typewriter, and began to write a book. All very fine while the daylight lasted, but when darkness fell there was the silence and the loneliness that made me regret that I had not heeded Kester's advice and stayed in Molyvos. It did not help to go into the town and eat at one of the tavernas along the waterfront. I was stared at and made to feel uncomfortable at being a woman alone. After a few unsuccessful sorties, I decided I would prefer to eat at home.

Someone in Athens had given me an introduction to the mayor, who invited me to the Greek equivalent of a cocktail party, where I met a number of the town's elite. Most of them spoke perfect English and my spirits rose. There were murmured mentions of future invitations, but none of them materialised. The mayor sent me an invitation to the opening of a new museum and there I met a charming urbane gentleman who, I subsequently learned, owned half the olive groves on Lesbos. We talked and I told him I was writing a book and, rather to my surprise, he asked would I like to come to his house to lunch next day. This was what I had been hoping for, and I said I would.

It was a great mistake. His wife took strong exception to the fact that I was there at her husband's invitation and, though she was icily polite, did little to conceal the fact that she was anything but pleased to see me. There was the usual black-clad widowed aunt in the drawing-room whose face set like a stone as I came in. She did not speak and, very pointedly, got up and left the room. The lunch was an uneasy meal, though the food was *haute cuisine* and served by two uniformed maids who eyed me with bright, inquisitive eyes. I was a curiosity, and felt increasingly ill at ease as the meal went on. That was my sole experience of high society in Mytilini, though I did meet some lesser beings as time went on.

There was the Englishwoman who claimed to be the reincarnation of the island's muse, Sappho, who had lived and sung her lyrics in 1612 BC, but I found it difficult to relate to her, as she dressed in a *chiton*, liked to play the lyre and was prone to reciting the verses of her ancestor at awkward times. Then there was the French governess who had spent the greater part of her life teaching the sons and daughters of the town's elite to speak French and English: she was alert, courageous and splendidly alive. Others of less stalwart stuff had packed and fled when the Germans invaded the island in 1944, but not Eileen Binou. She had remained with her adopted people, shared their privations and their suffering and thereby won their everlasting regard.

Somehow, she had gone scatheless through that grim time. As she said herself, 'They could not very well set up an internment camp for one lone Frenchwoman' and left her alone. When the war was over and the Communists were in control, they too spared her, but for a different reason.

'You see, I was French,' she said with a smile, 'a daughter of the Bastille.'

It was she who introduced me to Sophie, an English girl who was married to the heir of one of the island's wealthiest families. Greek marriages among the rich are seldom love matches, but are arranged with due regard to suitability, in other words, social status and, above all, marriage settlements. Sophie's had been celebrated in England where both she and her bridegroom were students at Cambridge University. Not daring to tell his parents, he had come back to the island for his vacations, but when he had taken his degree and a 'suitable' marriage was being planned for him, he had been forced to tell the truth.

One can only shudder at the thought of the uproar that must have followed. Poor Sophie was brought out to Lesbos, and her husband was conscripted into the army to begin his two years of compulsory service to the state. It would have been possible to buy him out and pay some penniless youth to take his place— this is often done in Greece—but no such clemency was shown to him, and Sophie was left to the mercy of her infuriated mother-in-law and the usual bevy of aunts. Mademoiselle Binou and I were sitting in one of the outdoor tavernas along the quay when she unexpectedly appeared, looking more distraught than usual.

There was a tiny church on the top of the hill that rises steeply above the town, which has a breathtaking view of the island and the distant Turkish coast, especially if one is there at sunrise, and that was where Sophie had been, only she had been indiscreet enough to be accompanied by a young Canadian man she had known in England. For that reason she had been shut in her room for more than a week. When she had threatened to throw herself out the window, she had been let out. She had come to say goodbye, as she was going back to England, and a divorce no doubt would be arranged on the grounds of her having deserted her husband.

Not long before that, I had been present when a young French girl had been curtly told to get on the plane to Athens that afternoon and be out of Greece within twenty-four hours. This took place in the foyer of the Lesbian Hotel and I overheard her angry protests and demands to be informed why she was being so abruptly expelled. Orders had come from Athens, she was told, and no details were given. I learned later that she was an artist who had come to paint some pictures of the island; whether she had more than tubes of paint in her luggage no-one seemed to know. This made me wonder if I would share her fate if it was discovered that I had spent a year in Soviet Russia and for four years had been a card-carrying member of the Communist Party in Australia. No-one had told me that Lesbos was known as the 'red Island', because at one time more than half the population were communists. The forces of reaction were now in power and memories were keen.

This, and poor Sophie's unhappy story, dampened my enthusiasm for all things Greek, and I was starting to regret I had signed a lease for six months when I met Christina.

She was sitting cross-legged on a stool in her cousin's general store, where I was trying to make known my needs in the limited Greek that I had learned.

'Need some help?' she asked. She spoke with a strong American accent though she looked Greek.

'You speak English! Thank heaven for that,' I said, immensely relieved. 'Where do you come from?'

'Boston,' was the reply. And so began a friendship that lasted till my lease ran out.

Christina was as much an alien in Mytilini as I was. Born of Greek parents who had migrated to Boston soon after they were married, she had spent the first thirty years of her life there. Then her father had died and nothing would satisfy her mother but a return to the place of her birth, an arid, ugly village hidden deep in the interior of the island.

'Mandemardos has to be seen to be believed,' Christina told me. 'One day I'll take you there to see for yourself.'

She did, and I did not wonder at the state of despair it had reduced her to. Her unhappiness had been so great that she grew ill, and her grim old mother had grown alarmed and agreed to live in Mytilini, where at least there was electric light and running water in the kitchen. But it was still a long way from Boston. Christina missed her job in the dental clinic, her girlfriends, the cheerful gossip round the soda bar, the movies, and the weekly dances at the club. Despite the difference in our ages, we had much in common, shared a common language, laughed at the same jokes, and agreed about the limitations of life in Mytilini.

When I fell ill with a severe attack of 'flu, what I would have done without Christina I do not dare to think. I was alone in the house, with no telephone with which to send out an appeal for help, and was beginning to have morbid thoughts about being found in an advanced state of decomposition when Chris arrived. She brought me food and medicine and even found a doctor who refused to come through the door for fear of catching the infection!

At her suggestion, when I had recovered I went to see the mayor and told him I planned to write a book about the island and needed some sort of transport to visit the more inaccessible parts. Publicity of any sort was welcome at the time, as the tourist industry was in its infancy and Lesbos, so far, had been overlooked. So a jeep and a driver were put at my disposal, and with Chris as a companion I went not only to Mandemados but to Agia Paraskevi, Kolloni, Moni Ipsilou, Sigri, and even to Eresos, where the immortal Sappho had been born—places where tourists rarely go.

With these explorations, and the book that started to take shape, the days passed pleasantly enough, but there was still that empty chair confronting me, the penetrating silence of the night. I hung a calendar on the wall and marked off every day as it went past and counted those that remained before I could go to Athens and catch a plane to London. I had learned that beauty and peace were not enough, not even on an island in the Aegean.

September came, and it was time to start packing up and worrying about what would become of my cats. There were two of them, orphans who had come uninvited but now were dearly loved.

The treatment cats receive in Greece is something best forgotten. They are looked upon as creatures of ill omen, worse than the evil eye or treading on a grave at midnight. To destroy a cat is to invite disaster, so no-one will be guilty of disposing of any of the poor detested creatures for fear of terrible reprisals. Rather let them starve, or even bury them alive; it is then God's will that they die; if it were not, He would save them. In the spring and autumn when their terrible fertility is at its peak, the air is filled with the piteous cries of starving kittens that have been thrown out of windows or over garden walls, abandoned in the parks and on the beaches—anywhere convenient—instead of being granted a swift and painless death.

It was with some misgiving, therefore, that I first saw Sissy sitting outside the door not long after I arrived in Mytilini. She had materialised out of the shadows, a full-grown cat, a patient, undemanding, grey and white nonentity who sat at the top of the stairs and stared at me with two enormous eyes, expressing neither hope nor expectation, just dumb resignation to an awful fate. It was not hard to guess where she had come from. The family that lived next door had gone to Australia to visit their son and daughter. They had simply locked the windows, slammed the door and left her to take care of herself. She was thin to the point of emaciation, her big head supported by a thin and wasted neck.

I gave her meat and a saucer of milk, but, famished though she was, she would not touch it until I had gone inside. She had no confidence in me at all, as the human race was her traditional enemy. As time went on she lost a good deal of her fear, though she would never let me touch her. A hand, to her, was something that delivered a blow, and when I tried to stroke her she would cower away. She would be waiting for me near the gate when I came back, however late the hour, and would race ahead of me along the path and sit at the top of the steps, purring with pleasure at seeing me again. I was glad of her company and the nights seemed to be less lonely.

Then we acquired Little Mo. I heard his cries one afternoon as I was returning from my daily swim. The cries were so loud and shrill that I thought a bird was trapped in the undergrowth and went to look and saw the tiny creature struggling to get free. He was perhaps a fortnight old; his eyes were open but his legs shook under him, his big head wobbled from side to side, and his terror was a pitiful thing to see.

I picked him up and tried to comfort him. At once the frantic cries were silent, and he nuzzled hopefully against my throat. Sissy, as usual, was waiting at the gate but for once I took no notice of her. The kitten's sides were hollow with starvation, and that was my first concern. Armed with a spoon and a saucer of milk, I wrapped him in a towel and took him on my knee. He sucked and gobbled greedily, and I felt the hollow sides begin to swell. At last he could take no more, so I wiped the milk off his face and set him on the floor. Deprived of the friendly hands, his former fears returned, and he began to bellow his distress. Immediately a grey and white form shot through the open door. It was Sissy, but a Sissy I had never seen before. Crouched low on the floor, alert, ears flattened to her head, she seized the kitten by the scruff of its neck and darted out the door. Amazed, and curious to see what she would do, I followed her, but by the time I reached the outside stairs she had disappeared. It took some time to find her hiding-place, and I eventually discovered her crouched behind a packing case.

The kitten was already nuzzling at her flank, its wee paws kneading busily, the faint hint of a purr in its tiny throat. Trying to conceal the kitten, Sissy shrank still further out of sight, staring up at me with wild, appealing eyes.

'Don't be afraid,' I told her. 'I won't take your baby from you.'

Here was the answer to my problem. The kitten had found a mother; he would sleep safe and snug at night, his face would be washed and his other needs attended to. I called him Little Mo because, like Pharaoh's daughter, I had found him among the bushes when I went to have a bathe.

Then, one morning, he had vanished. Sissy was there, but not behind the packing case; she sat perched on the garden wall, tail coiled neatly round her paws, an inscrutable expression on her face. I searched in every conceivable place while she looked on with what seemed like amusement. Suddenly, I was afraid. She had been in season for the last few days and certain evil visitors had been creating hideous sounds in the night. I looked at her accusingly. Had she allowed my pretty little orphan to be killed by one of those abominations while she indulged her wretched female instincts, leaving him unguarded and defenceless?

'Sissy! How can you sit there, looking so smug? Have you no feelings at all, you miserable, depraved, immoral creature?'

Sissy merely blinked her eyes, got up and stretched herself, then walked slowly round the corner of the house.

For two days I ignored her, gave her nothing to eat and shooed her away when she came to the kitchen door. Then I grew ashamed. Poor Sissy. Who was I to cast a stone? Filled with remorse, I hurried out and bought an extra lot of her favourite minced steak, but when I gave it to her her behaviour was so strange I thought that grief for Little Mo had unhinged her mind. Famished though she was, she only gulped down a few mouthfuls then, uttering a deep and mournful cry, she turned and dashed wildly out the door, down the stairs, and disappeared round the corner of the house. A few minutes later, she came back, ate a little more, and repeated the peculiar performance. A few minutes later, I looked out the door and found, to my utter disgust, that one of the hated suitors had taken advantage of her absence and was licking the final morsel off the plate. Thoroughly enraged, I sent him scurrying down the stairs by hurling a book at him.

Thus the lunatic phase set in. Each time I set down Sissy's plate of meat she would eat a little, utter her mournful cry and dash away, leaving it to the mercy of the lurking thieves next door. So I either had to grab the plate each time she disappeared or leave it where it was and let them devour the lot. This I was not prepared to do, so I collected an arsenal of stones and pieces of wood and hurled them at the marauders. I never scored a hit—they were far too quick and cunning.

Some weeks later, I was leaning out a window admiring the view of the sea, the sky, the distant coast of Turkey, when a sudden movement in the garden caught my eye, a flash of russet like a wind-blown autumn leaf. Without the least doubt, it was Little Mo.

Sissy was lying in a patch of shade, idly flicking her tail while he was frisking round her, looking very lean but strong and full of youthful *joie de vivre*. Scarcely believing my eyes, I ran downstairs, feeling that he had come back from the grave. As soon as she saw me, Sissy sprang to her feet and Little Mo took cover in the melon patch. It took me quite a time to find him, and when I did, I saw that every scrap of fur was standing on end and he was shuddering with fear, vainly trying to hide himself under a stone.

'What's the matter, you silly little thing?' I asked, bending down to stroke the quivering back. 'What are you afraid of. Don't you know me, Little Mo?' His only response was to thrust his head still further under the stone.

I picked him up. With a frenzied shriek, he sank his teeth in my wrist and tore my arm with his claws. Taken by surprise, I threw him violently away. He struck the wall with a thud, scrambled to his feet and scurried out of sight. At the sound of his terrified cry, Sissy had come bounding forward and I vented some of my feelings on her.

'Sissy, you little fool!' I hissed at her. 'What have you done to Little Mo? Why have you taught him to be afraid of me? Don't you know you'd both be dead if I hadn't taken care of you?'

Sissy stared at me unmoved and I went back upstairs to bathe and disinfect the long red scratches on my arm.

My ill humour did not last, as I was delighted to know that my pretty little pet was still alive and felt ashamed of having been so hard on Sissy. None knew better than she the menace of the courting male, and she had hidden him away so cunningly that neither they nor I had been able to find him. When he was strong enough to defend himself, she had permitted him to reappear. Now I understood the reason for her strange behaviour when I gave her food. Those hollow cries of hers had been her way of telling him to come and get his share. She must have carried scraps of meat in her mouth when she rushed out in such a crazy fashion, denying herself for him.

Her new pregnancy had possibly restored some of her milk, and by such means she had managed to keep him alive. Poor, devoted Sissy, and I in my blindness had thought she had gone mad.

But gone was the trusting little creature I had known. Mo was as wild and savage as a lynx cub, so I accepted this and took his food down to the garden, calling but making no attempt to find where he was hiding. Then I would return to the house and watch from an upper window. Almost at once, he would appear, and he and Sissy would dip eagerly into the dish. He was a greedy little male thing, jostling for the best position and the major portion of the meal, and she would draw back, blinking her eyes a trifle sadly, letting him eat his fill before she claimed her share.

Nothing could be more charming than the way he showed his love for her. He would rub himself backwards and forwards under her chin, snuggle against her side and lick her worn old face with an expression of the utmost tenderness, and she would sit with a look of bemused delight while he petted and made much of her.

Unexpectedly, I found I had to go to Athens and would be away for several days. There was no time to do anything but pack and catch the boat. Christina promised to come with food for my two castaways, and I left without any anxiety on their account. But when I returned there was no sign of either of them, and I wondered if Sissy had gone off hunting somewhere and if Mo had taken refuge under the house. I called a number of times, but he did not reply. It was getting dark when Sissy suddenly appeared at the kitchen door. She looked thin and ill, and I noticed that her shape had changed and knew that she had had her kittens while I was away. I peered down the stairs expecting to see the well-known shadow that was Little Mo, but no puckish face looked up at me, no plaintive meow answered my call. Sissy came instead, rubbing herself against my leg.

I searched the garden, I called and called, flashing the torch from side to side, hoping a familiar form would emerge from the shadows and put an end to my anxiety.

Christina told me that she had seen him two days before, but when she came to open up the house in preparation for my return, there was no sign of him. I could not believe that he was really gone, convinced that, as before, I would look out the window and see him flitting between the trees or playing in the melon patch. But day after day went past and there was no sign of my pretty ghost, my well-loved Little Mo. Then the woman next door gave me a clue.

'While you were away,' she said, 'the police have been busy

getting rid of the stray dogs. They're not fussy where they throw the baits. A friend of mine lost her pet poodle. Do you think that might have happened to your cat?'

And, suddenly, I knew. Sissy had found the bait while she was searching for beetles and lizards in the narrow lane outside the gate. Having found it, she would have hopped back over the wall, calling Little Mo to come and share the feast. It would not have occurred to her to eat it all herself, and it would also never occur to her to protest when he pushed her away until he had had his fill.

Perhaps there was only a mouthful or two for her, perhaps he had gobbled all of it down—how else account for the fact that she was still alive and he was not? Gentle, patient mother-creature that she was, she had destroyed him by her very act of self-denial.

There was no longer any need to carry food downstairs; Sissy waited outside the door each night and ate in the patch of light that fell across the porch. Sometimes she would look up and give her melancholy call, as though she, too, could not believe that there was no delicate red creature lurking in the shadows, waiting for me to go away.

October came, my trunks were packed and the last days on Lesbos had arrived. The rich hues of autumn were painting the sea and the hills a richer, deeper blue, and I would lean out the window and fill my eyes with the beauty I knew I might never see again. The pomegranate tree was laden with crimson fruit, the vine on the trellis was heavy with grapes, and the leaves on the melon patch had withered and turned yellow. Among these I saw something that I could not identify.

Immensely curious, I stole softly through the trees and parted the leaves. Snugly curled into a tight little ball were four half-grown kittens, fast asleep. They were plump and healthy, and undoubtedly Sissy's own. She had managed to conceal them all this time.

Magnificent Sissy! Splendid, undefeated, admirable Sissy! What would become of her after I had gone, I could not even guess, but I felt she would survive. She was indestructible.

CHAPTER 23

The final days arrived, accompanied by the usual turmoil that seems to be inescapable when such departures occur. Christina helped me cope with tax formalities, customs clearances, and currency conversion. She also solved the problem of what to do with unwanted books, clothes past their prime, and other surplus belongings, which she took away in a taxi to share with relatives and friends when I had gone.

There was no time to go to Molyvos, as I had planned to do, so Kester came to Mytilini and helped fasten the locks on trunks and nail packing-cases down. I walked with him to where the bus was waiting to take him back to Molyvos, neither of us mentioning that this might be the last time we would walk together for years, though it was in both our thoughts. I was contemplating a return to Australia, but he would remain in Greece.

Then came the last embrace, a few choked words, before the bus moved off and a final picture of a lean face smiling back at me, of clear blue eyes, and a fine hand raised in a gesture of farewell.

Christina said: 'We must have a party before you go.'

The 'party' consisted of Christina, her cousin Tucki and his wife and their little girl, George, another cousin, and myself. We met at one of the little outdoor tavernas that were perched precariously on the edge of the quay. Little wavelets lapped at our feet, a brisk wind flipped the tablecloth and disarranged our hair, and George, who drove the bus to Mandemados, filled our glasses with *retsina*.

Christina laughed, lifted her glass and banged it sharply on the table 'E-e-eyásus!' she cried before she raised it to her lips.

217

'E-e-eyásus!' we all answered, rapped our glasses on the table and drank. The party was under way.

'You're all lit up tonight. What's all this about?' I asked. She smiled.

'I've got a date tomorrow night, and I feel good.'

Ah, so my Christina had a beau! Sly minx, this was the first that I had heard of it. Whoever he was, I wished her well and hoped that he was worthy of her.

We were in the haunt of fishermen and sailors. None of the elite of Mytilini would have ever patronised the shabby little tavernas on the quay with their crude lights, bare concrete floors and the sweet smell of the sea.

A waiter brought us plates of food: fried fish, meat on a skewer grilled over an open fire, salad, crisp potatoes and another bottle of *ouzo*. Something told me I was going to enjoy myself. Tucki's wife Irene picked up a fork, carefully chose a piece of *kalamari*, added a crisp potato, looked at me and waited till I opened my mouth. Then she smiled and popped the food in. There were smiles on every face as hands reached across the table, and Tucki poured another round of drinks.

Christina acted as interpreter, doing her best to keep me aware of what was being said, but the pace increased and she was swept off on a tide of harmless jokes and friendly banter.

It was the hour when the fishing-fleet sets out to gather its nightly harvest in the channel between the island and the Turkish coast. I watched them cast off from their moorings and nudge their way towards the narrow opening in the mole, acetylene lanterns flaring on their prows, a line of phosphorescence trailing after them. It was a pretty sight. Then the engines of a gunboat began to throb and it slid after them.

'Going to protect the fishing-fleet from the Turks,' Christina said in an aside.

'See that building over there with "E.D.A." over the door?' she said another time. 'That's the headquarters of the Communist Party.' There was both awe and fear in her voice.

I remembered that Lesbos was known as a 'red island' because of its political past, and I thought of the French girl who had been so unceremoniously told to go, and the picture of a young man that I had seen on the front page of the *Athens News*. The face was one of classic beauty but the eyes had haunted me. His name was Gregory Damoutsidis and he had been caught red-handed while transmitting military and other vital information to Communist Bulgaria.

Greek counter-intelligence is confident of making mass arrests once they have obtained additional information which they are confident wil be disclosed,' the *Athens News* declared.

There was no need to wonder by what means the additional information would be obtained, and I had looked at the flawless face and wondered what it had become. It was not the face of a fanatic, but the face of a poet and a dreamer, with a suggestion of the martyr, and the eyes that stared out from the page were looking beyond the reader and into the hell he knew was awaiting him.

What had led him from his poet's dreams into the madhouse of politics? I wondered. What had induced him to barter his youth for the doctrine of destruction preached by men in a dark and brooding building marked with the symbolic E.D.A.? And what had he accomplished? What was his epitaph beyond a woman's thoughts as she sat silent among a group of laughing, carefree people? And the tears, no doubt, of the girl he had loved and the mother who had borne him?

'Come on! What's the matter with you? You're not with us.' It was Christina, leaning forward to peer in my face, calling me back from my thoughts.

The plates were empty and the *retsina* running low. Tucki's little girl was yawning and she leaned her head against her mother's arm. But this was not the signal to go home—far from it. It merely indicated that it was time to drain our glasses and move on to where gay music, songs, and the rhythm of dancing feet announced that further along the quay lively things were taking place.

We were greeted by a wild war-whoop from a maniac figure

wearing dirty cotton trousers, a sweat shirt and a rose behind one ear. He balanced a tray on one hand and wove airy arabesques with the other as he glided between the tables. He set the tray down with a final flourish before two sailors and some girls. They applauded him enthusiastically, upon which he bowed and turned his attention to us. Tucki was enveloped in a passionate embrace, Christina seized around the waist and whirled across the floor. Meanwhile, a tired woman near the stove rolled little fish in flour and dropped them into a pan of smoking oil.

A little of the noise had died away as we came in. We were the object of curious stares and a faint hint of hostility—Christina and I were so obviously foreigners—but as soon as Christina began to speak it was realised that she was Greek, and the tension eased. After we sat at a table and the mad proprietor brought us *ouzo* and *retsina*, the laughter and the songs commenced again. The music was traditional Greek, *bouzouki*, harsh and strident, possessing its own strange rhythm.

Tucki had had quite a lot to drink. Inspired by the beat of the music, he leaped to his feet and commenced one of the stately Greek dances that are all male posturing and frank display. Christina laughed, swayed a little in her chair and clapped in time to the music. The mad proprietor let out another yell and whirled across the floor, the rose now between his teeth, and several plates of fish and fried potatoes balanced along one arm, a highly skilled performance that aroused no response in his wife. She looked on and did not smile, mechanically rolling fish in the flour and dropping it into the pan.

Then Christina's other cousin, George, put down his glass, stood up and settled his belt more snugly round his waist, then stepped onto the floor. It was plain at once that George was no mean dancer. His shoes were heavy but they made no sound as they wove the complicated pattern of the dance, his eyes downcast, both arms nicely poised to balance the swaying movement of his hips and shoulders.

Tucki took Christina's hand and pulled her to her feet. The sailors banged their glasses on the table and the proprietor let out another ear-splitting yell, tossed a glass of *ouzo* down his throat, and wiped the perspiration off his face with a piece of greasy rag. Christina flirted the hem of her skirt and tossed her head while Tucki circled round her, advancing, retreating, hands outstretched to hover round her waist and hips but never touching, gliding away as she turned. And George danced on, intense and sombre, always alone.

Two of the sailors got up and commenced their own interpretation of the dance. Dressed in spotless white, lean hips emphasised by a black silk cummerbund, they seemed devoid of bones. Writhing and undulating, narrow loins out-thrust, they circled round each other, drawing close, retreating, eyes locked in a hypnotic stare, their lips parted. It was undisguised eroticism, something they had learnt in sleazy dives in Cairo, or it could be Singapore or even Liverpool. Tucki's little girl sat in her chair, wide-eyed and no longer sleepy, while Irene, smiling rather wanly, sat forgotten in her corner while the dance went on and on.

George held out his hand and pulled me to my feet. The music seemed to rise to a wilder, harsher pitch. One of the sailors hooked his arm through mine, Christina put her hand on Tucki's shoulder, and the second sailor followed suit so that we formed a chain and circled round and round until the music stopped and we all sank, breathless, into our chairs. Tucki's little girl now seized her opportunity.

'Papa, I want to dance,' she cried. 'Me! Me! I want to dance.'

Tugging her father's sleeve, she urged him back to the floor. He laughed and began the same slow gyrations he had used when dancing with Christina. The tiny girl threw back her head and shook her frilly skirt and then began to weave her hands and shoulders in the old and unmistakeable insinuation of the dance. Tucki played his part magnificently, pleading, cajoling, wooing, falling to his knees in front of her. It must be nice, I thought, to dance with a young and handsome father for your partner. Then she cast a scornful look at him and tossed her head and Tucki laughed and picked her up and carried her back to the table and put her in her mother's lap.

It was now past midnight. The tables along the quay were deserted, the chairs stacked up, the lights turned off. Tucki went to get his red Lambretta from the shed where he had left it early in the evening. When he came back, his wife mounted the pillion and put her arms around his waist and the little girl was hoisted onto the handle-bars, clasped his wrists in her hands and settled herself snugly against him.

Tucki kicked the engine noisily into life, and with a final wave and a last '*Chaireté*' they roared off into the night, leaving Christina, George, and myself on the quay.

All Mytilini seemed to be asleep. A cluster of lights far out to sea showed where the fishing-fleet was anchored off the coast of Turkey with the grey shape of the gunboat cruising watchfully around them. We walked together, arm-in-arm, and George's hand held mine in an urgent, painful grasp. Christina may have noticed, but she gave no sign, preoccupied perhaps with thoughts of the next night's rendezvous. The night whose day already tinged the sky.

I remembered what a poet I had met had said soon after I had come to Lesbos: 'Something happens in the nights on Lesbos in the months of summer. It is difficult to explain. You feel not yourself. You feel a wish to go into the pine grove and make love.'

It was now mid-August, high summer, and I knew what the poet meant. But nevermore, oh nevermore for me the scented pine grove, that had ceased on the night of the yellow fog.

George's eyes were heavy with reproach when I told him goodnight, kissed Christina, and walked away alone.

AN IMPROBABLE LIFE

BETTY ROLAND

I have already told how, in an idle hour, I made a list of the men who had made love to me and found they numbered sixty-four. That list, however, was inaccurate. It should have numbered sixty-five.

An Improbable Life is the first volume in the absorbing autobiography of Betty Roland, one of Australia's first women playwrights.

Born in the small Mallee town of Kaniva, in Victoria, Roland at eighty-five writes with refreshing candour of her life in Melbourne and her attempts at making writing a career. Her play *The Touch of Silk* was hailed in 1928 as 'the first Australian play written by a real dramatist', and Roland went on to write the script for Australia's first talkie.

Fleeing an unhappy marriage she ran away to England in 1932 with Guido Baracchi, a member of the Australian Communist Party, only to find herself in an equally complex web of deceit and personal intrigue. *An Improbable Life* is a unique excursion into a life of risk-taking, by a woman whose life and work spans the century.

CAVIAR FOR BREAKFAST

BETTY ROLAND

In 1933 Betty Roland went to Moscow with her lover Guido Baracchi, a member of the Australian Communist Party. Roland broke all the rules and stayed for fifteen months, sharing a room with fellow Australian writer Katharine Susannah Prichard.

Her diary details the excitement of her introduction to Russian theatre and her life in Moscow. She has a few privileges which almost compensate for the bedbugs and the fierce Russian winter. As Roland smuggles literature through Nazi Germany or stands in endless queues at 30 below zero, she experiences the false dawn of Stalin's new revolution. When she leaves in 1934, Stalin closes the country to the West.

Caviar for Breakfast follows Roland's first volume of autobiography *An Improbable Life,* in a setting that is both exotic and macabre.